"I believe every individu_____ _____ challenges should read this book. They will be encouraged and will come out victoriously! A must read for everyone whether you are a Christian or not. It will open your minds to see your life's struggles with a new perspective. I see a generation rising up from the ashes after reading this book. Simple yet profound and theologically sound. Like the Dr. Luke of the Bible, this is a thoroughly studied and Spirit-led book. This book will encourage you and embolden you to face your life's battles with boldness!"

—SAM ALEX B.E.(IT), M.DIV.,
Engineer turned preacher of the Gospel

"Nevin, in writing this book, has provided a powerful and compelling Scripture-based roadmap in identifying and dealing with spiritual warfare that we will all face in this life. He has taken what the world, the flesh and the Devil meant for evil and turned it into a blessing for those who read this book. It's my prayer that all who read this book will find mercy for their yesterdays, hope for today, peace for tomorrow and an unshakable faith filled with joy for their journey in life."

—PETE WEST

SPIRITUAL WARFARE

SPIRITUAL

NAVIGATING LANDSCAPES, OVERCOMING OPPRESSION,
AND LEARNING HOW TO BE VICTORIOUS

WARFARE

NEVIN WHITE

To my wife, Emily. Your love, support, and encouragement are invaluable. You are a gift from God and I love you.

CONTENTS

PART 1: SPIRITUAL LANDSCAPES

PART 2: SPIRITUAL OPPRESSION

PART 3: SPIRITUAL VICTORY

PART 1

SPIRITUAL LANDSCAPES

CHAPTER ONE

WE ARE AT WAR

*You armed me with strength for battle; you
humbled my adversaries before me.*

—PSALMS 18:39

One of the most difficult parts of life is understanding that
we are not immune to life's trials and tribulations. Even
Jesus Himself, during His ministry here on earth, said
that we will face trouble, but encourages us to take heart:
"I have told you these things, so that in me you may have
peace. In this world you will have trouble. But take heart!
I have overcome the world" (John 16:33). To understand
spiritual warfare, though, we must first acknowledge that
we are at war.

We are in a spiritual war fought in the spiritual realms
around us, but it manifests in our physical, mental, and
natural realms. Good versus evil. Satan and his dark forces
versus God, His angels, and followers of Christ. The Apostle
Paul wrote about this in Ephesians 6:12: "For our struggle
is not against flesh and blood, but against the rulers, against
the authorities, against the powers of this dark world and

against the spiritual forces of evil in the heavenly realms."
The famous theologian, C.S. Lewis, once wrote: "Like a good chess player, Satan is always trying to maneuver you into a position where you can save your castle only by losing your bishop."[1]

This book was birthed out of a season in my life while dealing with great adversity and fighting against spiritual warfare. It led me to an intense and ultimately enriching time with God and a time of searching Scripture to overcome my battles and trials. At first my battles were extremely disorienting, confusing, and disheartening.

You may be facing similar disorienting conditions and asking yourself a number of questions, such as *what caused it, how long will it last, and will God bring me out of it?* Maybe it is an attack on your health, career, finances, relationship(s) or another important area in your life. Sometimes a figurative or spiritual valley awaits or an opposing mountain. Perhaps it's a season of drought, wandering through the wilderness, or a proverbial giant standing before you, taunting and harassing you. What does the Bible say about overcoming these situations or seasons? I will cover that and also share part of my personal story with you in the coming chapters.

We will explore what the Bible says about "Spiritual Landscapes" in Part 1 (Valleys, Mountains, Wilderness, Exile), "Spiritual Oppression" in Part 2 (Fire, Giants, Storms), and "Spiritual Victory" in Part 3 (Prodigal, The Battle Within, The Armor of God, Victory). We will walk through each of these sections to navigate landscapes, overcome oppression, and learn how to be victorious! We will encounter Bible stories such as Ezekiel in The Valley of

Dry Bones, Elijah on Mount Carmel, the children of Israel in the wilderness, Daniel exiled in Babylon, David and Goliath, Jesus calming the storm, the Prodigal Son, and many more.

TRIALS AND ADVERSITY

But first, let's look at the broader concepts of trials, adversity, and what the Bible says about joy and hope. The world and society offer many different ways to cope with and combat challenges or adversity in our lives such as medication, counseling, vacation, hobbies, time with family, and the list could go on. As a physician I can tell you none of these things are inherently bad. But in this mindset, we tend to see our struggles in non-spiritual terms and as a result, we tend to seek non-spiritual solutions. Some people even engage in harmful behavior or develop addictions as a coping mechanism, such as alcohol, drugs, overeating, or even compulsive shopping, which are not healthy alternatives. The Bible instructs us to praise God when tests and challenges come at us from all sides; to count it as a sheer gift. Scripture provides a guide on how to approach these spiritual battles and persevere despite adversity.

James 1:2-3 says, "consider it pure joy, my brothers and sisters, whenever you face trials of many kinds, because you know that the testing of your faith produces perseverance." Do you praise God in your trials? Do you praise God before your breakthrough? Are you joyful when trouble comes your way? What does James, the brother of Jesus, mean by this? First, we must understand that the Book of James is about how to live a mature Christian life and how to respond in difficult times. Shortly after the start of the early Christian Church there was persecution of Christians and they left Jerusalem and were scattered throughout the surrounding areas and beyond. James stayed in Jerusalem and wrote to the scattered believers to guide and encourage them on how to live life as mature believers. In this set of verses, above, James is saying we will face trials. Not *if* but *when* we will face trials. God can use these trials to grow us, mature us, build us, and ultimately draw us closer to Him.

HOPE IN THE TRIALS

In his letter to the Romans, The Apostle Paul wrote that sufferings produce perseverance which leads to character and subsequently hope. "Not only so, but we also glory in our sufferings, because we know that suffering produces perseverance; perseverance, character; and character, hope" (Romans 5:3-4). It may seem paradoxical or counter-intuitive that our trials, adversity, and battles could lead to hope. What does Paul mean by this? He goes on in verses 5 – 8 (paraphrased) to explain that Christ came and died for sinners and God's love has been poured out through the Holy Spirit, who has been given to us. This is good news! We have hope because Jesus died for us and we have direct access to the Holy Spirit. Paul expounds on this concept of hope later in his letter to the Romans:

> For everything that was written in the past was written to teach us, so that through the endurance taught in the Scriptures and the encouragement they provide we might

have **hope**. May the God of **hope** fill you with all joy and
peace as you trust in him, so that you may overflow with
hope by the power of the Holy Spirit.

—ROMANS 15:4, 13

Our hope is placed in the One who was abandoned and
killed on the Cross. The road to Calvary was not glamorous and our road in following Jesus won't always be
glamorous either. The fact is, in this world we will have
trouble. Following God doesn't remove all the obstacles.
We have to stand firm. We need unwavering faith because
"the thief comes only to steal and kill and destroy" (John
10:10). We need divine determination, so that similar to
Paul, we can say "none of these things move me" (Acts
20:24 NKJV). Hold on to the promise that Christ gives
us through relationship with Him that you "may have life
and have it to the full" (John 10:10).

I am not a theologian, pastor, Bible scholar, historian,
or anything of the like. However, I felt *compelled* or what
some would say "led" or "called" to write this book. Have
you ever felt like there was something you had to do or
wanted to do, or you would have missed an opportunity to
serve God and help others? Something deep in your soul
driving you forward. The question, however, is, what is it
that compels us? In 2 Corinthians 5:14, Paul proclaims
a beautiful statement, "for it is the love of Christ that
compels us." May this book bless you and give you fresh
perspective and revelation. Above all, may this book give
glory to God and "may the words of my mouth and this
meditation of my heart be pleasing in our sight, Lord, my
Rock and my Redeemer" (Psalms 19:14).

CHAPTER TWO

VALLEYS

*Every valley shall be filled in, every mountain
and hill made low. The crooked roads shall
become straight, the rough ways smooth. And
all people will see God's salvation.*

We often glorify the high times and places in our lives, such
as birthdays, graduations, weddings, babies, or holidays.
However, if we are honest, truly reflect and analyze our lives,
it is often the valley or low places that catapult us further
in faith in Christ, growing us in areas that we didn't realize
needed growth. You may even find yourself in the midst of
a valley right now. You would prefer a peak or mountain
top experience to teach you similar lessons, but, nonetheless,
you have found yourself in a valley, sometimes at your own
doing, or perhaps you don't know how you ended up there.
The Bible refers to a number of different literal valleys, and
while these are important locations, here we are discussing
figurative or spiritual valleys and seasons in life.

THE VALLEY OF THE SHADOW OF DEATH

The Psalmist David wrote the following regarding the valley of the shadow of death:

> The Lord is my shepherd, I lack nothing. He makes me lie down in green pastures, he leads me beside quiet waters, he refreshes my soul. He guides me along the right paths for his name's sake. Even though I walk **through the darkest valley**, I will fear no evil, for you are with me; your rod and your staff, they comfort me. You prepare a table before me in the presence of my enemies. You anoint my head with oil; my cup overflows. Surely your goodness and love will follow me all the days of my life, and I will dwell in the house of the Lord forever.
>
> —PSALMS 23

Some translations refer to it as the *darkest* valley; others the valley of the shadow of death. Notice it is not the valley of death, but the valley of the shadow of death. An intense or scary experience, nonetheless, but we will escape death or harm as the Lord is our Shepherd, who guides and leads us along right paths. He can comfort us with His rod and staff and even prepare a table for us in the presence of our enemies. He will protect us and bless us and cause overflowing of abundance in our lives. With that said, the valleys in our lives can still feel very real and challenging.

THE VALLEY OF DRY BONES

A passage in Ezekiel 37 details the Old Testament prophet,

Ezekiel, and his encounter with God in a valley, classically titled "The Valley of Dry Bones":

> The hand of the Lord was on me, and he brought me out by the Spirit of the Lord and set me in the **middle of a valley**; it was full of bones. He led me back and forth among them, and I saw a great many bones on the floor of the valley, bones that were very dry. He asked me, "Son of man, can these bones live?" I said, "Sovereign Lord, you alone know." Then he said to me, "**Prophesy to these bones** and say to them, Dry bones, hear the word of the Lord! This is what the Sovereign Lord says to these bones: I will make breath enter you, and you will come to life. I will attach tendons to you and make flesh come upon you and cover you with skin; I will put breath in you, and you will come to life. Then you will know that I am the Lord." So, I prophesied as I was commanded. And as I was prophesying, there was a noise, a rattling sound, and the bones came together, bone to bone. I looked, and tendons and flesh appeared on them and skin covered them, but there was no breath in them. Then he said to me, "**Prophesy to the breath;** prophesy, son of man, and say to it, This is what the Sovereign Lord says: Come, breath, from the four winds and breathe into these slain, that they may live." So, I prophesied as he commanded me, and breath entered them; they came to life and stood up on their feet—a vast army.
>
> —EZEKIEL 37:1-10

In this passage, immediately we see that Ezekiel was placed in the valley by the Lord and he is surrounded by dry bones. God knew the bones could live, but He wanted to see Ezekiel's response and involve him as an active participant in the valley experience, grow his faith, and reveal something to him. God was commanding Ezekiel to "prophesy" or speak to the dry bones and subsequently God would bring them to life. Ezekiel did as he was commanded, and God formed the bones and bodies together. But one thing was still missing – the breath, or the Holy Spirit. Ezekiel "prophesied" and spoke to the breath and it entered the bones and bodies and they came to life and stood up on their feet, a vast army. This is a picture of the people of Israel and God was telling Ezekiel to prophesy to them and tell them God would bring them back to the land of Israel.

We see that at first God placed Ezekiel exactly where He wanted him, to listen and dialogue, but then Ezekiel had to prophesy or speak. God wants us to get alone with Him, to listen and dialogue. Romans 10:17 says, "consequently, faith comes from hearing the message, and the message is heard through the word about Christ." Our faith is built by listening to and reading the Word, but then we must prophesy over our lives with what He is speaking to us or what His Word is speaking to us. We see that sometimes God is the one who places us in the valley, as was the case with Ezekiel, to teach us to listen and speak. Less of an attack, more of a divine appointment. Some valley seasons can certainly be an attack from Satan or spiritual warfare, to discourage or deter us from our destiny. Or perhaps we are in a valley because of our own doing and we have to climb our way out of the muck and mire with God's help. Whatever the case, God can work on us in the valley so that He can subsequently work *through* us when out of the valley.

RESURRECTING DRY BONES

I'm reminded of another story in Scripture where God raised dry bones from the dead...Lazarus. In this intriguing and heartbreaking story, turned miraculous and triumphant, Jesus showed up at the tomb of Lazarus, the brother of Martha and Mary, and raised Lazarus from the dead. The story takes place in John 11, where we see that Martha and Mary were in their own valley, a valley of despair, pain, loss, and grief. Their brother, Lazarus, fell ill and died. They initially sent for Jesus to come heal Lazarus from his illness, but when He didn't come as soon as they would have liked, tragedy struck, or so they thought.

After being summoned, Jesus stayed where He was for two more days and then eventually showed up to Bethany and met with Martha and some of the others who were present. "On his arrival, Jesus found that Lazarus had already been in the tomb for four days" (John 11:17). Martha and Mary both shared their grief with Jesus and their regret that He wasn't present to heal Lazarus in time. Tears were shed, even Jesus wept, and the following scene occurred:

> Jesus, once more deeply moved, came to the tomb. It was a cave with a stone laid across the entrance. "Take away the stone," he said. "But, Lord," said Martha, the sister of the dead man, "by this time there is a bad odor, for he has been there four days." Then Jesus said, "Did I not tell

you that if you believe, you will see the glory of God?" So they took away the stone. Then Jesus looked up and said, "Father, I thank you that you have heard me. I knew that you always hear me, but I said this for the benefit of the people standing here, that they may believe that you sent me." When he had said this, Jesus called in a loud voice, **"Lazarus, come out!"** The dead man came out, his hands and feet wrapped with strips of linen, and a cloth around his face. Jesus said to them, "Take off the grave clothes and let him go."

—JOHN 11:38-44

Jesus showed up at the tomb of Lazarus and raised him from the dead, even though it had already been four days, which was a significant amount of time. Lazarus' sisters and the Jewish people present shared their concerns with Jesus and He in turn showed them the glorious resurrecting power of God. Perhaps this was a foreshadowing of Jesus' own resurrection. Despite their initial disappointment in Jesus (or so it seemed), they shared their hearts with Him. They leaned into His grace and He showed them compassion. They could have sent Jesus away or been angry or given up, but instead they chose to lean in. Like the sisters and people in the story, we all at some point have or will experience the heart wrenching loss of a loved one or some other tragedy. Most of us may experience the loss of a job, income, or some other significantly negative or challenging thing in our lives. It is in these seasons or moments, the valleys of life, that we have to present our pain, grief, and disappointment to the One who can take it, the One who can heal us, the Savior of us all...Jesus.

THE VALLEY OF OBEDIENCE AND BLESSING

Sometimes we may just be passing through a valley onto the next location or season in our lives. As was the case with the children of Israel while marching towards the Promised Land, they marched through a valley between two opposing mountains, Mount Gerizim and Mount Ebal. It was from these two mountains, respectively, that the priests yelled out blessings if the people kept the covenant and curses if the covenant was broken. It was a way for God and the priests to emphasize the importance of keeping the covenant with God as they marched forward. In Deuteronomy 28 we see blessings were promised for obedience:

> If you fully obey the Lord your God and carefully follow all his commands I give you today, the Lord your God will set you high above all the nations on earth. All these **blessings** will come on you and accompany you if you **obey** the Lord your God. You will be blessed when you come in and blessed when you go out.
>
> —DEUTERONOMY 28:1-2, 6

The Children of Israel were marching through a valley and were reminded of their covenant with God and the blessings that may ensue if the covenant was kept. Sometimes when we are in a valley season, perhaps God is simply reminding us of our covenant with Him and His subsequent blessings for our obedience. Or reminding us of the trouble and harm that will come upon us if we do not keep the covenant. Of course, Paul wrote: "There is now no condemnation for those who are in Christ Jesus" (Romans

13

8:1). We are not saved by our works and we can't earn God's favor or lose His favor. However, it is better to be in the will of God and to seek and honor Him. Galatians 6:9 says, "let us not become weary in doing good, for at the proper time we will reap a harvest if we do not give up."

THE VALLEY OF BACA

The Children of Israel passed through another valley on their way to the Promised Land, the Valley of Baca, which means the valley of weeping, brokenness, loss, or grief. "As they pass through the valley of Baca, they make it a spring; the rain also covers it with pools. They go from **strength to strength**" (Psalms 84:6-7 NKJV). As we pass through valley seasons, we, too, go from strength to strength. With God's strength in our time of need, perhaps our valleys will become springs of joy, success, and spiritual enlightenment.

While in a personal valley season, God began to show me these valley stories and concepts in the Bible. As I continued to study valleys, mountains, and other spiritual landscapes in the context of spiritual warfare, I decided to write this book. I included Scripture and my personal experiences here and throughout the book to hopefully encourage others through their own spiritual warfare and help them overcome spiritual oppression and have spiritual victory in their lives.

As I sought God and His Word, He began to highlight specific verses and speak to me via repetition. In seasons in my life when I seek Him diligently, God often uses repetition as emphasis to drive a point home. In other words, Scripture was repeated in more than one venue or source throughout a given day or period. The first verse that God gave to encourage me, as someone prayed it over me: "No weapon formed against you shall prosper, and every tongue which rises against you in judgment you shall condemn" (Isaiah 54:17 NKJV). What a powerful prayer and verse as it helped begin the slow ascent from my valley of despair.

Romans 8:28 says, "and we know that in all things God works for the good of those who love him, who have been called according to his purpose." God works for our good and we are called for His purpose, no matter the season or the valley. When God gives you a word, it can change your perspective. Everything we face in life, good or bad, is knitted with a purpose. What a great reminder that was for me in my time of need. Often, we get hung up on why we are in a valley, but whatever the reason we can know that is the beautiful thing about pain; He promises it for our good and for His glory.

CHAPTER THREE

MOUNTAINS

Many peoples will come and say, "Come, let
us go up to the mountain of the Lord, to the
temple of the God of Jacob. He will teach us
his ways, so that we may walk in his paths."
The law will go out from Zion, the word of
the Lord from Jerusalem.

—ISAIAH 2:3

Throughout the Bible, mountains are extremely significant in their geographical location and context. Similar
to valleys, mountains may have several different meanings
whether that be literal, figurative, or spiritual. Abraham
climbed a mountain to offer Isaac as a sacrifice (Genesis
22). Moses climbed Mount Sinai and received the Ten
Commandments (Exodus 32). Moses was the embodi-
ment and deliverer of the Old Testament law from God
to the people. We saw in Chapter 2, as the children of
Israel passed by Mount Gerizim, the priests yelled out
blessings that correlated to keeping the covenant with God
(Deuteronomy 28). Obedience led to blessings. Mountains

in the Old Testament were significant places of worship, sacrifice, and blessings.

We also see in the New Testament that mountains or high places were a significant place of Jesus' ministry. Some believe that Mount Gerizim was the same mountain in the New Testament that Jesus met the woman at the well and proclaimed Himself as "living water and a well of eternal life." A Samaritan woman came to draw water and Jesus asked her for a drink:

> The Samaritan woman said to him, "You are a Jew and I am a Samaritan woman. How can you ask me for a drink?" (For Jews do not associate with Samaritans). Jesus answered her, "If you knew the gift of God and who it is that asks you for a drink, you would have asked him, and he would have given you **living water**." Jesus answered, "Everyone who drinks this water will be thirsty again, but whoever drinks the water I give them will never thirst. Indeed, the water I give them will become in them a spring of water **welling up to eternal life**."
>
> —JOHN 4:9-10, 13-14

In a similar declaration, during the Sermon on the Mount, Jesus said, "blessed are those who **hunger and thirst for righteousness**, for they will be filled" (Matthew 5:6). Jesus was also on a mountain for the "transfiguration." "After six days Jesus took with him Peter, James, and John, the brother of James, and led them up a **high mountain** by themselves. There he was transfigured before them. His face shone like the sun, and his clothes became as white as the light" (Matthew 17:1-2). It was on Golgotha, which was more of a hill than a mountain, significant, nonetheless, that Jesus was crucified for the sins of mankind: "Carrying his own cross, he went out to the place of the Skull (which in Aramaic is called Golgotha). There they crucified him, and with him two others—one on each side and Jesus in the middle" (John 19:17-18).

OVERCOMING MOUNTAINS

We often think of mountain tops or peaks as pinnacles or high points in our lives, which certainly may be an accurate analogy at times. However, in terms of spiritual warfare, occasionally we will see that mountains may actually represent adversity or obstacles to climb or overcome. One way to climb or overcome spiritual mountains is to utilize intercessory or intervention prayer. We do this by *invoking* Jesus' name against the "mountains" and by praying and proclaiming God's Word and promises over our lives. It is in the name of Jesus that we have authority and power when we pray such as the Apostle Peter, when he invoked Jesus' name to heal the lame beggar at the Beautiful Gate:

> When he saw Peter and John about to enter, he asked them for money. Peter looked straight at him, as did John. Then Peter said, "Look at us!" So, the man gave them his attention, expecting to get something from them. Then Peter said, "Silver or gold I do not have, but what I do have I give you. **In the name of Jesus Christ** of Nazareth, walk." Taking him by the right hand, he helped him up, and instantly the man's feet and ankles became strong.
>
> —ACTS 3:3-7

Pastor Jentezen Franklin once said in a sermon, "the most powerful avenue of prayer is when you say, 'Father I come in the name of Jesus and I plead the blood of the lamb.'"[1] Pastor Jim Cymbala, in his book *Fresh Wind, Fresh Fire* exclaimed, "The name of Jesus, the power of his blood, and the prayer of faith have not lost their power over the centuries."[2] As we see here, to have effective, powerful, mountain moving prayers we must invoke the name of Jesus and plead the blood of the lamb!

Earlier in Acts, just before His ascension to heaven, Jesus said the following to the disciples, "but you will receive power when the Holy Spirit comes on you; and you will be my witnesses in Jerusalem, and in all Judea and Samaria, and to the ends of the earth" (Acts 1:8). In Acts 2 they received the Holy Spirit on the day of Pentecost and went forth preaching, teaching, and healing by this power. We, too, have access to the same Holy Spirit. Paul said that the same power that raised Jesus from the grave lives in us. He wrote: "The Spirit of God, who raised Jesus from the dead, lives in you" (Romans 8:11 NLT) and "I also pray that you will understand the incredible greatness of God's power for us who believe him. This is the same mighty power that raised Christ from the dead and seated him in the place of honor at God's right hand in the heavenly realms" (Ephesians 1:19-20 NLT).

PRAYER AND FASTING

Effective prayer may require utilization of a few other disciplines, such as fasting, persistence, repetition, and consistency. Jesus mentioned the power of prayer and fasting to the disciples in Matthew 17. The disciples unsuccessfully tried to heal a demon-possessed boy, who suffered with seizures, and they brought the boy to Jesus for help. After driving out the demon, the following happened:

> Then the disciples came to Jesus privately and said, "Why could we not cast it out?" So Jesus said to them, "Because of your unbelief; for assuredly, I say to you, if you have faith as a mustard seed, you will say to this mountain, 'Move from here to there,' and it will move; and nothing will be impossible for you. However, this kind does not go out except by **prayer and fasting**."
>
> —MATTHEW 17:19-21 NKJV

It is by faith and especially through prayer and fasting that we drive out evil spirits, break addictions, and move the "mountains" in our lives. In a similar teaching, later in the chapter, Jesus tells His disciples, "also you can say to this mountain, 'Go, throw yourself into the sea,' and it will be done. If you believe, you will receive whatever you ask for in prayer" (Matthew 21:21-22). We have to believe (have faith) to receive what we ask for in prayer; believe it to receive it.

There are several examples in the Old Testament and New Testament where breakthroughs came after prayer and fasting such as Nehemiah, Esther, Jehoshaphat, and the apostles in Acts. Some examples of exhortation to fasting:

> "Even now," declares the Lord, "return to me with all your heart, with **fasting and weeping and mourning**." Rend

your heart and not your garments. Return to the Lord your God, for he is gracious and compassionate, slow to anger and abounding in love, and he relents from sending calamity.

—JOEL 2:12-13

Then your light will break forth like the dawn, and your healing will quickly appear; then your righteousness will go before you, and the **glory of the Lord will be your rear guard**. Then you will call, and the Lord will answer; you will cry for help, and he will say: Here am I. "If you do away with the yoke of oppression, with the pointing finger and malicious talk."

—ISAIAH 58:8-9

A prominent example of prayer and fasting is seen in Daniel 10, where Daniel fasted and prayed for 21 days and God moved on his behalf. He said for three weeks, "I ate no choice food; no meat or wine touched my lips" (Daniel 10:3). After this a man showed up and met Daniel at the bank of the Tigris river, who was thought to be an angel and said to him:

"Daniel, you who are highly esteemed, consider carefully the words I am about to speak to you, and stand up, for I have now been sent to you." And when he said this to me, I stood up trembling. Then he continued, "Do not be afraid, Daniel. Since the first day that you set your mind to gain understanding and to humble yourself before your God, **your words were heard**, and I have come in response to them. But the prince of the Persian kingdom resisted me twenty-one days. Then Michael, one of the chief princes, came to help me, because I was detained there with the king of Persia."

—DANIEL 10:11-13

The angel told Daniel that he came in response to Daniel's humility and desire for understanding. It also appears that he came in response to Daniel's prayer, fasting, obedience, and persistence. This passage gives us another insight into spiritual warfare in the heavenly realms. The angel was resisted by the "prince of the Persian kingdom," but Michael, the Archangel, had to help the angel break through. Now, with prayer and fasting, Daniel had his breakthrough and got his word from God.

CLIMB A MOUNTAIN

Sometimes we have to climb a spiritual "mountain" to overcome it. Other times we have to climb a literal mountain to pray. Again, mountains are very significant locations in the Bible, as was the case with Elijah on Mount Carmel:

And Elijah said to Ahab, "Go, eat and drink, for there is the **sound of a heavy rain**." So, Ahab went off to eat and drink, but Elijah climbed to the top of Carmel, bent down to the ground and put his face between his knees. "Go and look toward the sea," he told his servant. And he went up and looked. "There is nothing there," he said. Seven times Elijah said, "Go back." **The seventh time** the servant reported, "**A cloud** as small as a man's hand is rising from the sea." So, Elijah said, "Go and tell Ahab, 'Hitch up your chariot and go down before the rain stops you.'" Meanwhile, the sky grew black with clouds, the wind rose, a **heavy rain** started falling and Ahab rode off to Jezreel. The power of the Lord came on Elijah and, tucking his cloak into his belt, he ran ahead of Ahab all the way to Jezreel.

—1 KINGS 18:41-46

Elijah was an Old Testament prophet and the nation was in its third year of a severe drought and famine. Elijah had previously prophesied this drought and now was prophesying an end to the drought. He heard the sound of *heavy rain*, he hadn't seen rain yet, but he prophetically knew it was coming and told King Ahab to get ready. After he climbed Mount Carmel and kneeled to the ground, he continued to pray persistently for breakthrough and sent his servant to the sea who kept reporting back no rain. Elijah never looked up. He wasn't relying on what he saw, but what he heard and already believed would come true. On the seventh time his servant reported a cloud the size of a man's hand and Elijah knew, despite being small, this cloud was the start of something big. The rain was coming!

As we learn from Elijah, we will often hear or sense things in the spiritual realm, before we see them. God will often give us a word, before it comes to fruition. The writer of Hebrews wrote: "Now faith is the substance of things hoped for, the evidence of things not seen" (Hebrews 11:1 NKJV). Paul wrote to the Corinthians: "For we walk by faith, not by sight" (2 Corinthians 5:7 NKJV). After we hear the word from God, we have to *speak* it. Paul wrote to the Romans: "God, who gives life to the dead and calls those things which do not exist as though they did" (Romans 4:17 NKJV). In other words, speak those things that are not as though they already are. I'm not saying we can speak whatever we want into existence or as some say, "name it and claim it" or follow the "prosperity gospel." However, I am saying if we get a word from God and it lines up with His Word and His plans, then we can believe by faith that it will come true and stand on His promises.

In our own lives we may not see the breakthrough at first. It may take some time and when it comes it may be small initially. Look for it. Don't miss it. Stay focused. Be patient. Continue to pray and worship your way through the waiting. The breakthrough or miracle may also require repentance, turning from our ways, refocusing on God and making Jesus Lord of our lives. God may be working on us before He changes the circumstances. He may be delaying our deliverance in order to transform us, grow us, and build us into the Image of Christ.

Additionally, as we saw in Elijah's case, repetition and consistency were key. He sent his servant to the sea *seven times* before the cloud formed. Seven is the number of completion in the Bible and reminds me of the children of Israel marching around Jericho seven times before the walls fell and Naaman dipping in the Jordan River seven times before his leprosy was healed. All cases show obedience, repetition, and consistency. According to James: "Elijah was a human being, even as we are. He prayed earnestly that it would not rain, and it did not rain on the land for three and a half years. Again, he prayed, and the heavens gave rain, and the earth produced its crops" (James

5:17-18). James was reminding us that Elijah was just a man. But he prayed, and when he prayed, mighty things happened. We, too, have the ability to pray like Elijah and see breakthrough in our own lives, if we pray earnestly.

PERSONAL MOUNTAIN

One day, during the process of studying spiritual land-scapes and writing this book, I realized that I was staring a "spiritual mountain" in the face; a large obstacle to over-come. I felt led to pray for breakthrough at the *Praying Hands* statue on Oral Roberts University (ORU) campus. When I arrived, I was surprised to see the following verse inscribed on the large statue: "Death is swallowed up in victory" (1 Corinthians 15:54 NKJV). I had already been thinking about that verse on the way, as it was in the same passage as the "verse of the day." As I prayed at the *Praying Hands*, it was as if God was saying, "you will have victory over your mountain, your season, because Jesus has already overcome." God gives us victory through Jesus' name!

After pondering and meditating on these truths, I then felt drawn to pray at a church nearby. I didn't know who I would run into or what would happen, but I knew I should go, and God would show up in a tangible way. As I walked into the church's prayer room, I noticed this Scripture immediately: "You will be blessed when you come in and blessed when you go out" (Deuteronomy 28:6). I read through the full passage, prayed there for some time and went home for the evening. Later, while listening to a sermon online, a pastor mentioned this same passage from Deuteronomy about blessings. I was immediately encouraged by this and took it as another sign that God was speaking. Some things might seem coincidental, but God often uses repetition to get our attention. If you are seeing the same theme, message, word or phrase being used, God may be speaking to you or confirming things to you. Take time to listen and look for repetition.

In the beginning of this project, I kept remembering the story of Elijah and the "cloud the size of a man's hand." It was a small cloud. A small start. A small victory. However, as I began applying this and other Biblical principles to my life, I knew change and victory would come through the process.

CHAPTER FOUR

WILDERNESS

*Just as Moses lifted up the snake in the
wilderness, so the Son of Man must be lifted up.*

—JOHN 3:14

The "wilderness" is one of the most prominent spiritual
landscapes discussed in the Bible, especially in context
of the children of Israel's 40 years or Jesus' 40 days in
the wilderness. Wilderness is defined as "a tract or region
uncultivated and uninhabited by human beings. An obso-
lete, wild, or uncultivated state."[1] Wilderness is often used
in context to deserts or wasteland. In terms of spiritual
landscape and spiritual warfare, wilderness may also be a
time of separation or exile (see Chapter 5 Exile) or a time
of unfortunate or challenging circumstances. A time of
testing, refining, or growth, where we ultimately have to
lean on God and the Holy Spirit.

ELIJAH IN THE WILDERNESS

Just after God granted the prophet Elijah victory on Mount

Carmel in 1 Kings 18 (see Chapter 3 Mountains), Elijah then ran away to the wilderness. Elijah prayed fervently for rain on Mount Carmel, the rain came, the drought ended, and the miracle happened. However, right after that, Jezebel sent a messenger to Elijah to threaten him. As a response, "Elijah was afraid and ran for his life. When he came to Beersheba in Judah, he left his servant there, while he himself went a day's journey into the wilderness. He came to a broom bush, sat down under it and prayed that he might die" (1 Kings 19:3-4).

An angel of the Lord woke Elijah up two separate times from his sleep in the wilderness and gave him bread and water. "Strengthened by that food, he traveled forty days and forty nights until he reached Horeb, the mountain of God. There he went into a cave and spent the night. And the word of the Lord came to him: 'What are you doing here, Elijah'" (1 Kings 19:8-9)? Interestingly, Elijah left the wilderness and ended up at another mountain, but now was hiding in a cave. The Lord continued to speak to him and said, "go out and stand on the mountain in the presence of the Lord, for the Lord is about to pass by" (1 Kings 19:11).

As Elijah was standing on the mountain, the Bible says a powerful wind came through, an earthquake happened, and then a fire, but the Lord was not in the wind, earthquake, or fire. It goes on to say, "and after the fire came a **gentle whisper**" (1 Kings 19:12). The Lord spoke to Elijah in a gentle whisper and He commanded Elijah to go anoint three men, one of which was Jehu, who later defeated Jezebel, and one of which was Elisha, who took up Elijah's prophetic mantle.

What an interesting story, especially on the heels of the miracle on Mount Carmel in 1 Kings 18. We saw that God was doing miracles through Elijah one minute, and he appeared to be on top of the world, but then he was running for his life the next minute. On top of the mountain one minute, hiding in the wilderness the next. Before we judge Elijah, are we too different in our own spiritual battles? We saw that an angel of the Lord sustained Elijah in the wilderness and strengthened him for travel to a different mountain to meet with God. Even despite this next miracle, being fed by an angel, Elijah was still afraid of Jezebel and hid in a cave. He was a man *on the run*. But God showed up and we see that it was a "gentle whisper."

One way to view this story is that, due to fear, Elijah didn't reach his full prophetic potential. This could be an incorrect assessment, but it certainly could be considered. We can apply this to our own lives and our own ministries. When God calls us, we should follow His leading, even if we find ourselves in a wilderness or mountain season, even if we are afraid, even if all we hear is a "gentle whisper." God will continue to do His prophetic miracles in us and through us if we let Him. If we refuse to do the will of the Lord, for the Kingdom of God, perhaps He will find someone else who will.

THE CHILDREN OF ISRAEL

The children of Israel's wilderness experience started after leaving Egypt. They spent 40 years in the wilderness under Moses' leadership and this journey stands out as a trying time in Israel's history, but also as a significant time in

Biblical history. The people of Israel started in Egypt initially under Joseph's tenure as second in command to Pharaoh, during a famine. They left their homeland and went to Egypt for food and protection, but ended up staying for over 400 years, most of that time spent as slaves to Pharaoh and the Egyptians. They went to Egypt initially for a blessing and it became a burden.

God eventually used Moses to free the people from Egyptian oppression (remember the ten plagues) and guided them out to the Red Sea. Egypt is a picture of slavery and bondage and can be a picture of spiritual bondage in our lives today. Interestingly, they had to go the long way around the Philistine armies to the Red Sea. When Pharaoh let the people go, God did not lead them on the road through the Philistine country, though that way would have been shorter. For God said, "if they face war, they might change their minds and return to Egypt" (Exodus 13:17). When God takes us the long way around, it's not because He is trying to withhold anything from us. It's often to prepare us and protect us for the blessing He has for us. The long way around with God is better than the shortcut without God. He knew they weren't ready for the battle; He knew they would want to return to Egypt, despite the slavery and bondage. Sometimes we're not so different.

After God took them out and around, He took them *through*. "By day the Lord went ahead of them in a pillar of cloud to guide them on their way and by night in a pillar of fire to give them light, so that they could travel by day or night" (Exodus 13:21). He parted the Red Sea, they crossed over, the waters went back to their original form and crushed Pharaoh and his army that was pursuing the Israelites. God will take us through and will defeat our enemies. God gave them bread to eat along the journey through the wilderness and "the people of Israel called the bread manna" (Exodus 16:31). He also guided them with an angel that went before them: "See I am sending an angel ahead of you to guard you along the way and to bring you to the place I have prepared" (Exodus 23:20). Although, the plot thickened. They were supposed to go onto the Promised Land, but complaining, grumbling, bad attitudes, and lack of faith in God cost them 40 years in the wilderness.

May we not let complaining, grumbling, poor attitudes, or lack of faith cost us our mission, focus, and destiny in serving God and others. Paul wrote this to the Philippian church: "I know what it is to be in need, and I know what it is to have plenty. I have learned the secret of being content in any and every situation, whether well fed or hungry, whether living in plenty or in want. I can do all this through him who gives me strength" (Philippians 4:12-13). Proverbs 18:21 says, "the tongue has the power of life and death, and those who love it will eat it's fruit." We have to speak *life* over ourselves and learn to be content in any and every situation and lean on Christ who gives us strength.

JOSHUA AND THE PROMISED LAND

After God took the children of Israel out of Egypt and across the Red sea, they spent 40 years in the wilderness. Moses and an entire generation never made it to the Promised Land. They made it to the proverbial finish line in the journey but failed to make it across. Their complaining cost them their destiny. What a tragedy. However, Moses' successor, Joshua, finally took the next generation of Israelites across the Jordan River, the finish line, and into the Promised Land. It was not an easy process getting across the Jordan River and many battles were subsequently fought afterwards to claim the land that God had promised them. However, God was with them through the way and we, too, need to realize that sometimes the blessing is in the battle. In every hardship, Jesus meets us, refines us, encourages us, and strengthens us.

Initially, after God instated Joshua as the new leader, He had to instill confidence in him. God said to Joshua, "no one will be able to stand against you all the days of your life. As I was with Moses, so I will be with you; I will never leave you nor forsake you" (Joshua 1:5). God encouraged him to keep the Word on his lips and meditate on it day and night: "Keep this Book of the Law always on your lips; meditate on it day and night, so that you may be careful to do everything written in it. Then you will be prosperous and successful" (Joshua 1:8). Over and over in Joshua Chapter 1, God repeatedly encouraged Joshua: "Have I not commanded you? Be strong and courageous. Do not be afraid; do not be discouraged, for the Lord your God will be with you wherever you go" (Joshua 1:9).

Just like Joshua, if we want to be prosperous and successful, we must speak the Word over our lives and meditate on it. God tells us He will never leave us nor forsake us, to be strong and courageous, and that He will be with us wherever we go. To win our spiritual battles, to cross into our own promised land, we must lean on God and His Word, and take heart that He will be with us. "So do not fear, for I am with you; do not be dismayed, for I am your God. I will strengthen you and help you; I will uphold you with my righteous right hand" (Isaiah 41:10). "The Lord is my light and salvation; Whom shall I fear? The Lord is the strength of my life; Of whom shall I be afraid" (Psalms 27:1 NKJV)?

As I continued to study and write about the concept of spiritual landscapes, I further identified with each of the proverbial locations of valleys, mountains, wildernesses, etc. God used Joshua 1:9 as an encouragement through what seemed to be my own spiritual wilderness. Isaiah wrote: "Forget the former things; do not dwell on the past. See, I am doing a new thing! Now it springs up; do you not perceive it? I am making a way in the wilderness and streams in the wasteland" (Isaiah 43:18-19). Sometimes God will take us into the wilderness, where the water is dried up, just to redirect us to the *Source*, and He will make a way. Jesus said, "whoever believes in me, as Scripture has said, rivers of living water will flow from within them" (John 7:38). I began to realize God may have had me in a wilderness for a reason, despite its rough terrain, God was working in me, drawing me to the Source, and a new spring was coming forth.

JESUS TESTED IN THE WILDERNESS

In Scripture, the number forty often represents testing or trials. The children of Israel spent forty years wandering in the wilderness, thwarted by their own complaints and iniquities. Jesus spent forty days in the wilderness, tempted by the Devil, but He overcame by fasting and using Scripture. "Jesus was led by the Spirit into the wilderness to be tempted by the devil. After fasting forty days and forty nights, he was hungry" (Matthew 4:1-2). Notice, it was the Holy Spirit who led Jesus into the wilderness to be tempted by the Devil. In spiritual warfare, we face three adversaries or three temptations – the lust of the flesh, the lust of the eyes and the pride of life:

The tempter came to him and said, "if you are the Son of God, tell these stones to become bread [**lust of the flesh**]." Jesus answered, "It is written: Man shall not live on bread alone, but on every word that comes from the mouth of God."

Then the devil took him to the holy city and had him stand on the highest point of the temple. "If you are the Son of God," he said, "throw yourself down. For it is written: He will command his angels concerning you, and they will lift you up in their hands, so that you will not strike your foot against a stone [**the pride of life**]." Jesus answered him, "it is also written: Do not put the Lord your God to the test."

Again, the devil took him to a very high mountain and showed him all the kingdoms of the world and their splendor [**the lust of the eyes**]. "All this I will give you," he said, "if you will bow down and worship me." Jesus said to him, "Away from me, Satan! For it is written: Worship the Lord your God and serve him only." Then the devil left him, and angels came and attended him.

—MATTHEW 4:3-11 (EMPHASIS MINE)

The children of Israel were not able to overcome the enemy in the wilderness, but Jesus did. Jesus engaged with the Devil in spiritual warfare, one-on-one in open territory, and He won through prayer and fasting. After this forty day fast in the wilderness, after overcoming Satan, Christ, clothed in God's Spirit, was able to go on and start His ministry. When going to the Cross, Jesus knew He had already defeated Satan. And He knew He could beat him again and subsequently overcome death. But it wasn't until He went through the wilderness that He was ready to start His ministry, and ultimately die for the sins of the world. The wilderness prepared Him for the spiritual battles ahead and enabled Him to step out into His destiny on earth.

If you find yourself in a wilderness season, be encouraged! God has not forsaken you. Instead, He is preparing you. John Bevere wrote: "If we are to step into the fullness of what God has planned for us, we must be willing to leave our comfort zone and pursue the way that God's Spirit leads. This path will often take us through what the Bible refers to as a wilderness. This is where God causes new life to spring forth."[3] God can use the wilderness to guide, restore, strengthen and prepare us, and it is often out of these seasons that ministry is birthed.

STRENGTH IN WEAKNESS

So how do we find strength and purpose in our wilderness season? The Apostle Paul went through a trial and endured a personal "thorn in his flesh" for many years and explained that it was to keep him humble, to help him rely on God and His strength:

> Therefore, in order to keep me from becoming conceited, I was given a thorn in my flesh, a messenger of Satan, to torment me. Three times I pleaded with the Lord to take it away from me. But he said to me, "My grace is sufficient for you, for my power is made perfect in weakness." Therefore, I will boast all the more gladly about my weaknesses, so that Christ's power may rest on me.
>
> —2 CORINTHIANS 12:7-9

According to Paul, sometimes trials, spiritual battles, wilderness terrain, or other hardship seasons may be there to expose our weaknesses, to humble us, and help us rely on God's direction and strength. He goes on to say, "that is why, for Christ's sake, I delight in weaknesses, in insults, in hardships, in persecutions, in difficulties. For when I am weak, then I am strong" (2 Corinthians 12:10). Christ is revealed in our weaknesses; His strength can become our strength.

Since our weaknesses can reveal His strength, then we can also be molded into what He wants to do in us and through us, despite hardships. Paul says, "but we have this treasure in jars of clay to show that this all-surpassing power is from God and not from us. We are hard pressed on every side, but not crushed; perplexed, but not in despair; persecuted, but not abandoned; struck down, but not destroyed" (2 Corinthians 4:7-9). We are jars of clay to be molded for His purposes. Despite our external struggle, we persevere.

Regarding our weaknesses, the writer of Hebrews wrote:

> For we do not have a high priest who is unable to empathize with our weaknesses, but we have one who has been tempted in every way, just as we are – yet he did not sin. Let us then approach God's throne of grace with confidence, so that we may receive mercy and find grace to help us in our time of need.
>
> —HEBREWS 4:15-16

Earlier we saw that Jesus had been tempted in every way in the wilderness, and also throughout His ministry. He overcame the temptations and subsequently overcame the Cross for us. He is able to empathize with our weaknesses and we can come to Him in our time of need. He came in flesh and identified with us so that in turn we can identify with Him and come to Him in confidence. "God will be no more eager to act tomorrow than he is right now. He is waiting for us to take his promises seriously and go boldly to the throne of grace. He wants us to meet the enemy at the very point of attack, standing against him in the name of Christ."[2] We can approach God in our wilderness season and let Him help us and fight for us. That is powerful, and we need to understand that God may be using our own wilderness seasons to guide, restore, and strengthen us. He may be getting us ready to minister to others and so much more.

CHAPTER FIVE

EXILE

*Consequently, you are no longer foreigners
and strangers, but fellow citizens with God's
people and also members of his household.*
—EPHESIANS 2:19

The word exile means "the state or a period of forced absence from one's country or home."[1] 1 Peter 2:11 speaks of Christians as exiles in this world, for though we are citizens of the heavenly Kingdom, we are right now living in a foreign land. We can look to Daniel's exile to Babylon and John's exile to the island of Patmos as guides for our own pilgrimage in difficult times. Both of these stories represent captivity, but more specifically John's island exile may also represent isolation. Islands can be literal and figurative representations of isolation. Have you heard the phrase, "I feel like I'm on an island?" If you have ever lived through a period of isolation, such as separation from people or society, then you can probably relate to this. We can look at both Daniel and John's experiences to see how to live in exile.

EXILE TO BABYLON

Daniel was an Old Testament prophet that was taken into captivity while living in Jerusalem in 605 BC. In Daniel Chapter 1, the king of Babylon, Nebuchadnezzar, destroyed the city of Jerusalem, and took many of the people into captivity back to the city of Babylon, including Daniel and some of his closest friends. Even though the Babylonians tried to indoctrinate Daniel and his Israelite friends into the Babylonian culture and customs, they stayed firm in their own convictions and customs to serve God in a place that defiled Him, even to the end.

One example of Daniel's faithfulness to God is where we get our present-day "Daniel Fast." Daniel and his counterparts outperformed the other men by choosing only vegetables and water over the king's food, that was not considered appropriate for Jewish people to eat. We see their reward: "At the end of the ten days they looked healthier and better nourished than any of the young men who ate the royal food. So, the guard took away their choice food and the wine they were to drink and gave them vegetables instead" (Daniel 1:15-16). Because of this, Daniel and his friends were shown favor: "To these four young men God gave knowledge and understanding of all kinds of literature and learning. And Daniel could understand visions and dreams of all kinds" (Daniel 1:17).

FAITH DESPITE ADVERSITY

In Daniel Chapter 3, we see the story of Daniel's friends' humility and faithfulness to serve God during their time in

Babylon, despite exile and adversity. "King Nebuchadnezzar made an image of gold, ninety feet high and nine feet wide and set it up on the plain of Dura in the province of Babylon" (Daniel 3:1). The king mandated that all would bow down to the ground, at the sound of the musical instruments, to worship the gold statue that he had set up. Daniel's three friends, Hananiah (Shadrach), Mishael (Meshach) and Azariah (Abednego) refused to worship the empire and their integrity and commitment to God landed them in a fiery furnace heated *seven times* over. But God delivered them, and they were exalted by the king to a place of great blessing and influence.

In Daniel Chapter 6, some of King Darius' satraps and administrators tricked him into issuing a decree against prayer to anyone other than the king. When they caught Daniel praying to God three times per day, as he had always done, they convinced King Darius to uphold the decree and Daniel was placed into a lions' den, facing imminent death. However, King Darius did not wish harm upon Daniel and rushed to the lions' den early the following morning and called out to Daniel to see if God had rescued him from the lions:

> Daniel answered, "May the king live forever! My God sent his angel, and he shut the mouths of the lions. They have not hurt me, because I was found innocent in his sight. Nor have I ever done any wrong before you, Your Majesty." The king was overjoyed and gave orders to lift Daniel out of the den. And when Daniel was lifted from the den, no wound was found on him, because he had trusted in his God.
>
> —DANIEL 6:21-23

END OF EXILE

In Daniel Chapter 12, the last chapter of the book, King Cyrus of Persia sent Daniel's people, the Israelites, back to Jerusalem ending the 70-year exile in Babylon, as predicted in the Book of Jeremiah. Jeremiah 29:11 is often quoted and applied to encourage us in our lives for God having a plan to prosper us and not to harm us, which is certainly true, however, in full context it was initially given to the people of Israel:

> This is what the Lord says: "When seventy years are completed for Babylon, I will come to you and fulfill my good promise to bring you back to this place. For I know the plans I have for you," declares the Lord, "**plans to prosper you and not to harm you**, plans to give you hope and a future. Then you will call on me and come and pray to me, and I will listen to you. You will seek me and find me when you seek me with all your heart. I will be found by you," declares the Lord, "and will bring you back from **captivity**. I will gather you from all the nations and places where I have banished you," declares the Lord, "and will bring you back to the place from which I carried you into **exile**."
>
> —JEREMIAH 29:10-14

Daniel remained faithful to God throughout his exile in Babylon, through his tenure with multiple kings, and through much adversity. Then the book says this in Daniel 12:3: "Those who are wise will shine like the brightness of the heavens, and those who lead many to righteousness,

like the stars for ever and ever." What a powerful statement! Paraphrased it says those who are wise and those who lead many to righteousness, will shine like the stars in the sky. Not providing power, wealth, or any prowess to one's own righteousness, but through humility, wisdom, and seeking the kingdom of God. Through the belief in Jesus Christ and our service to Him, may we shine our light before men, no matter what land or kingdom we find ourselves living in at present.

This reminds me of another verse or statement in the Bible, but this time in the New Testament. Fast forward, many years later, the Apostle Paul wrote: "Do everything without grumbling or arguing, so that you may become blameless and pure, children of God without fault in a warped and crooked generation. Then you will **shine among them like stars in the sky** as you hold firmly to the word of life" (Philippians 2:14-16). Paul was encouraging the church at Philippi and subsequently the Church of present day to be humble, don't argue, become blameless and pure, despite the world around us, despite our spiritual battles, and, therefore, shine like stars in the sky. Again, not of ourselves, but focusing on the Kingdom of God, belief in Jesus Christ, no matter what generation, time period, or earthly kingdom, and in doing so we will shine like stars – we will be a light to others. The Gospel of Matthew says: "Let your light so shine before men, that they may see your good works and glorify your Father in heaven" (Matthew 5:16 NKJV).

EXILE TO PATMOS

The Book of Revelation was written by the Apostle John while exiled to the Island of Patmos. Both books, Daniel and Revelation, contain significant prophecy for the future, including the end times. Revelation means "a surprising and previously unknown fact, especially one that is made known in a dramatic way"[2] or "the divine or supernatural disclosure to humans of something relating to human existence or the world."[2] Revelation is meant to bring understanding.

The book of Revelation is a revealing of Jesus Christ in glory. Revelation 1:1: "The revelation from Jesus Christ, which God gave him to show his servants what must soon take place." Jesus is introduced as the Ruler of kings and it is a story of the return of the King to establish His Kingdom. In verse 9, John began his writing of the vision he received from Jesus and explained that he "was on the island of Patmos because of the word of God and the testimony of Jesus." In verse 19, Jesus told John, "write, therefore, what you have seen, what is now and what will take place later."

In Revelation Chapters 2 and 3, John wrote about seven churches in Asia Minor, letters that described what Jesus thought about these churches, and some today believe these churches also correlate to the church age from first century to today. The rest of the Book of Revelation is spent detailing what will take place in the future and end times prophecy, such as the rapture of the Church, the seven-year Tribulation period, the Antichrist, the Millennial Kingdom, and the New Heaven and New Earth. These prophecies, detailed by Jesus through John, are filled with imagery, symbolism, and important details about the Kingdom of God and the future of the Church, our future.

REVELATION WARFARE

I encourage you to read the entire Book of Revelation, if you haven't already, and see what God reveals to you through the process. However, for this chapter we will focus on spiritual warfare and how it can relate to our lives. Specifically, Revelation Chapter 12 details the fight in heaven, long ago, of Michael and the angels versus Satan, the dragon, and how he was cast down to earth:

> Then war broke out in heaven. Michael and his angels fought against the dragon, and the dragon and his angels fought back. But he was not strong enough, and they lost their place in heaven. The great dragon was hurled down—that ancient serpent called the devil, or Satan, who leads the whole world astray. He was hurled to the earth, and his angels with him.
>
> —REVELATION 12:7-9

Satan was triumphantly defeated and cast out of heaven. We see how it was done: "They triumphed over him by the blood of the Lamb and by the word of their testimony; they did not love their lives so much as to shrink from death" (Revelation 12:11). Shortly after this, the dragon (Satan) was enraged at the woman (Israel) and her offspring: "Then the dragon was enraged at the woman and went off to wage war against the rest of her offspring—those who keep God's commands and hold fast their testimony about Jesus" (Revelation 12:17).

This is true for us today, in our spiritual warfare, against Satan and his evil forces. We are the offspring of Israel and Abraham and are those that "keep God's commands and hold fast their testimony about Jesus" (verse 17 above). Our testimony about Jesus is what gets us attacked by Satan, the deceiver, liar, and accuser. He comes only to steal and kill and destroy. It is also true, however, that we can triumph over Satan and sin by the blood of the Lamb (Jesus) and by the word of our testimony. We can win the spiritual battles over Satan, because Jesus has already won the war, as long as we trust in Him and utilize the power and authority of His name. In the Gospel of Luke, Jesus put it this way: "I saw Satan fall like lightning from heaven. I have given you authority to trample on snakes and scorpions and to overcome all the power of the enemy; nothing will harm you" (Luke 10:18-19).

While in my personal wilderness, mentioned last chapter, and what felt like a personal exile, I continued to seek God and write this book and spiritual breakthrough continued. It was time to come out of exile and move forward into the next season God would have for me, but the good fight was still raging. I was reminded of this promise: "'You will seek me and find me when you seek me with all your heart. I will be found by you,' declares the Lord, 'and will bring you back from captivity'" (Jeremiah 29:13-14). After He brought me through each of the spiritual landscapes' valleys, mountains, wildernesses, and was bringing me out of exile, then the next phase of the book began. It was time to write about overcoming spiritual oppression.

PART 2

SPIRITUAL OPPRESSION

CHAPTER SIX

FIRE

You let people ride over our heads; we went
through fire and water, but you brought us to
a place of abundance.

−PSALMS 66:12

Fire is a significant symbol and is used in many different ways throughout the Bible. In the Old Testament, fire often represents God's divine presence, such as the burning bush from which God spoke to Moses: "There the angel of the Lord appeared to him in flames of fire from within a bush. Moses saw that though the bush was on fire it did not burn up" (Exodus 3:2). Here, fire is a manifestation of God Himself, for Moses turned away from the sight "because he was afraid to look at God" (vs 6). Ezekiel's vision: "He looked like fire; and brilliant light surrounded him" (Ezekiel 1:27). Fire can also be used for guidance. The children of Israel were guided through the wilderness: "By day the Lord went ahead of them in a pillar of cloud to guide them on their way and by night in a pillar of fire to give them light, so that they could travel by day or night" (Exodus 13:21). These Scriptures represent God's presence, glory, and direction to His people for what I call the "guiding fire."

THROUGH THE FIRE

In spiritual warfare, however, it may not seem like a guiding fire, but instead "passing through the fire." The heat is turned on and no one likes that feeling! It happens when there are pressures to conform, to succumb to the weight of it all. Remember when Daniel's three closest friends and confidants, Shadrach, Meshach, and Abednego, experienced the heat being turned on them? They were thrown into a literal fire for refusing to bow down to King Nebuchadnezzar's statue of gold. Talk about having a bad day! The king brought them forward and exclaimed, "if you do not worship it, you will be thrown into a blazing furnace. Then what god will be able to rescue you from my hand" (Daniel 3:15)? But their response to the king was epic:

> King Nebuchadnezzar, we do not need to defend ourselves before you in this matter. If we are thrown into the **blazing furnace**, the God we serve is able to deliver us from it, and he will deliver us from Your Majesty's hand. But even if he does not, we want you to know, Your Majesty, that we will not serve your gods or worship the image of gold you have set up.
>
> —DANIEL 3:16-18

They could have easily bowed down to what was wrong, but they made a defining decision to stand up for what was right. They had faith that God would rescue them despite the fire or "faith through the fire." They knew God was able to rescue them from the hand of Nebuchadnezzar, but even if He didn't, they refused to worship anyone but the one true God. This takes a bold, next level type of faith! If we can understand and strive for this type of faith, then we know that despite our trials and adversity, God can rescue us and even if He does not, we will remain faithful to Him, because He remains faithful to us. His ways are higher than our ways, His thoughts are higher than our thoughts (see Isaiah 55:9).

How does the story of Shadrach, Meshach, and Abednego end? King Nebuchadnezzar in his furious rage turned up the fire seven times hotter than usual and threw them into the fire. It was so hot that the flames of the furnace killed the soldiers nearby. Then King Nebuchadnezzar said, "look! I see four men walking around in the fire, unbound and unharmed, and the fourth looks like a son of the gods" (Daniel 3:25). The king called them out of the fire and when they came out the bystanders "saw that the fire had not harmed their bodies, nor was a hair of their heads singed; their robes were not scorched, and there was no smell of fire on them" (Daniel 3:27). Then Nebuchadnezzar said:

Praise be to the God of Shadrach, Meshach and Abednego, who has sent his angel and rescued his servants! They trusted in him and defied the king's command and were willing to give up their lives rather than serve or worship any god except their own God. Therefore, I decree that the people of any nation or language who say anything against the God of Shadrach, Meshach and Abednego be cut into pieces and their houses be turned into piles of rubble, for no other god can save in this way.

—DANIEL 3:28-29

They experienced a *miracle* in the fire. God showed up and walked with them through the fire, saving them from the hand of King Nebuchadnezzar and the blazing flames. They were willing to give up their lives rather than compromise their faith in God. This brought glory and honor to God in all of Babylon, the largest and most powerful nation at the time. If they had compromised their faith, they would have forfeited their testimony. But God delivered them through the fire and to God be the glory! When He delivers us through the fire, may we, too, give Him the glory. May He receive honor and praise through our testimony. The true test is trusting God while in the middle of the fire, that He will deliver us before He has done it.

This is what the prophet Isaiah had to say about passing through the fire: "When you pass through the waters, I will be with you; and when you pass through the rivers, they will not sweep over you. When you walk **through the fire**, you will not be burned; the flames will not set you ablaze. For I am the Lord your God, the Holy One of Israel, your Savior" (Isaiah 43:2-3). As with the people of Israel, so it will be with us. Isaiah is not saying *if* you walk through the fire, but *when*. Peter wrote: "Dear friends, do not be surprised at the fiery ordeal that has come on you to test you, as though something strange were happening to you" (1 Peter 4:12). We will endure the fire as we walk through it, but the trials in our lives will not consume us because God promises to be with us. When we pass through wildernesses and valleys, they will develop springs of water; when we pass through rivers or fire, they will not consume us.

TONGUES OF FIRE

Just prior to His ascension, Jesus commanded the apostles, "do not leave Jerusalem, but wait for the gift my Father promised, which you have heard me speak about. For John baptized with water, but in a few days, you will be baptized with the Holy Spirit" (Acts 1:4-5). After Jesus' ascension, the apostles were all in the Upper Room during Pentecost, and they experienced the following:

> Suddenly a sound like the blowing of a violent wind came from heaven and filled the whole house where they were sitting. They saw what seemed to be **tongues of fire** that separated and came to rest on each of them. All of them were filled with the Holy Spirit and began to speak in other tongues as the Spirit enabled them.
>
> —ACTS 2:2-4

Notice that they heard the sound of a violent or *rushing wind*, it filled the house, and then they saw "tongues like fire" and were filled with the Holy Spirit. They heard it and then they saw it. As we've discussed in other areas of this book, you often hear things in the spiritual realm before they manifest in the physical realm, and then you see them. Interestingly, the Holy Spirit was represented here with symbolism of "tongues of fire."

Shortly after they had received the Holy Spirit at Pentecost, Peter stood up and gave his first sermon to the crowd gathered there. He began, "fellow Jews and all of you who live in Jerusalem, let me explain this to you; listen carefully to what I say" (Acts 2:14). After his sermon: "Those who accepted his message were baptized, and about three thousand were added to their number that day" (Acts 2:41). Jesus said the Holy Spirit would come, it came, and Peter was emboldened to address the crowd. The same Peter who denied Jesus three times prior to His crucifixion now preached the Gospel to thousands and they responded in great number. Jesus said He would build His Church on the rock (see Matthew 16:18). Now the Church had indeed begun, but not until the Holy Spirit came like *fire*.

Not long after this in Acts 4, the believers prayed the following:

> "Now, Lord, consider their threats and enable your servants to speak your word with great boldness. Stretch out your hand to heal and perform signs and wonders through the name of your holy servant Jesus." After they prayed, the place where they were meeting was shaken. And they were all filled with the Holy Spirit and spoke the word of God boldly.
>
> —ACTS 4:29-31

This is another instance where the Holy Spirit showed up and filled the group. They were asking for the ability to speak the Word with great boldness and for God to perform signs and wonders. Through the Holy Spirit and the name of Jesus they wanted to go out and do bold ministry for the Kingdom of God. The Holy Spirit kept showing up and empowering them to spread the Gospel and grow the early Church. May we pray for the same *boldness* in our own lives and in our own ministries and may the Holy Spirit lead, guide, and empower us to speak the Word of God boldly. This is paramount for overcoming spiritual warfare and gaining ground while fighting the good fight.

REFINING FIRE

As we go through trials or through the fire, sometimes it is meant for our good, to refine us. A refiner's fire does not consume or destroy, it refines and purifies. Fire removes impurifications from metals, thereby leaving the specific metal's purest and most useful form. So, it is when the Holy Spirit is working on us, refining us, and purifying us. The Apostle Peter put it this way:

> In all this you greatly rejoice, though now for a little while you may have had to suffer grief in all kinds of trials. These have come so that the proven genuineness of your faith—of greater worth than gold, which perishes even though **refined by fire**—may result in praise, glory and honor when Jesus Christ is revealed.
>
> —1 PETER 1:6-7

Even though we have to suffer grief and trials, they have to happen in order to prove the genuineness and authenticity of our faith, resulting in praise, glory, and honor to Jesus. Peter went on to say, "though you have not seen him, you love him; and even though you do not see him now, you believe in him and are filled with an inexpressible and glorious joy, for you are receiving the end result of your faith, the salvation of your souls" (1 Peter 1:8-9). Because of our faith in Jesus, we are able to experience inexpressible and glorious joy, despite the trials. The end result of our faith is salvation of our souls. There is purpose in the battle and purpose in the refining fire.

Similar to the concept and revelation above, the Apostle Paul wrote this to the church in Corinth:

> If anyone builds on this foundation using gold, silver, costly stones, wood, hay or straw, their work will be shown for what it is, because the Day will bring it to light. It will be revealed with fire, and the fire will test the quality of each person's work. If what has been built survives, the builder will receive a reward.
>
> —1 CORINTHIANS 3:12-14

One day all of our work here on earth will be revealed with fire and it will test the quality of our work. Whatever is unnecessary, evil, or not useful for the Kingdom of God will be burned up in the fire, but whatever is done for the Kingdom, and for Jesus, in pure devotion will remain. We are saved by grace through faith and not by works; however, our good works will result in a reward in heaven. Genuine salvation is entirely of God and it results in an expression of good works and a changed life.

Even if the fire seems to have burned up all things around us, God is *still* with us. We may feel as though we are consumed in the fire, but the Lord comes as a refiner's fire and not as a forest fire. "For I the Lord do not change;

therefore you, O Children of Jacob, are not consumed" (Malachi 3:6 ESV). This is God's covenant with us, and He has confirmed it and sealed it with Jesus' blood. Jesus said, "and surely I am with you always, to the very end of the age" (Matthew 28:20). Even if you think you have failed, that you will never rebound, or that you have "burned it all to the ground," that is simply not true with Jesus. God can "make beauty from ashes" (see Isaiah 61:3) and He can "restore the years" (see Joel 2:25).

As with Moses and the burning bush, the children of Israel and the pillar of fire, God will guide us with His presence, most often through the conduit of the Holy Spirit. By faith, He will protect us through the fire as with Shadrach, Meshach, and Abednego in the fiery furnace. "He will never leave us or forsake us" (see Hebrews 13:5). He will refine us with *fire* and through the Holy Spirit. We will become more like His Son, Jesus, and be transformed more and more into His Image.

CHAPTER SEVEN

GIANTS

I can do all this through him who
gives me strength.
—PHILIPPIANS 4:13

Do you have a giant standing before you, taunting you or insulting you? We all encounter giants at one time or another in our lives. Giants represent large, difficult issues, circumstances, or problems that seem like they won't go away or ever resolve.[1] They could be something that developed recently or have been there for a long time. They could be something you have already tried to overcome or perhaps, because of fear, you've avoided at all cost. One thing to realize is that we all have giants. We all face seemingly, insurmountable obstacles, problems or temptations. So how do we face our giants? We will look to a few prominent stories from the Bible for answers on how to deal with figurative or spiritual giants in our own lives.

WHAT IS YOUR GIANT?

Your giant could be fear, anxiety, or depression. It could be a relationship that is at odds or giving you grief. It could be an addiction, habit, or personal characteristic that you want to overcome, such as alcohol, drugs, cigarettes, lust, pornography, etc. It could be a prodigal son or daughter that you are worried about being away from God. It could be some sort of potential damage, such as legal, financial, career or reputation trouble.[1] Whatever your problem is, identify it now before it is nurtured, fed, or even encouraged into something bigger. I will pause briefly and say this chapter is not the end all authority on this topic. If you are facing a giant, I encourage you to seek professional help, either from a pastor, counselor, doctor, family member, or others where appropriate and applicable, depending on your issue.

DAVID AND GOLIATH

The most prominent and well-known "giant" seen in the Bible is undoubtedly Goliath. David, his opponent, was one of the most prominent and greatest kings of Israel. However, when David went up against Goliath, he was just a young shepherd boy and hadn't yet reached his full king status. Saul was still in place as king of Israel; Saul and the Israeli army were lined up against Goliath and the Philistine army. Goliath was taunting Saul and the Israeli army and David was tending to his sheep in a field, far from battle. David's father sent him to bring food to his brothers who were lined up at the battlefield. When

David arrived, he heard Goliath taunting the Israeli army, challenging them to match one of their soldiers against him. Even though Goliath stood head and shoulders above other men, David was perplexed as to why no one was going out to fight this Philistine giant and defend Israel.

David, who was too young to join the battle lines, volunteered to fight Goliath: "He took his staff in his hand, chose five smooth stones from the stream, put them in the pouch of his shepherd's bag and, with his sling in his hand, approached the Philistine" (1 Samuel 17:40). Goliath moved towards David, saw that he was only a boy and was insulted. Goliath hurled threats at David, and he responded, "you come against me with sword and spear and javelin, but I come against you in the name of the Lord Almighty, the God of the armies of Israel, whom you have defiled. This day the Lord will deliver you into my hands and I'll strike you down and cut off your head" (1 Samuel 17:45-46). Others had measured Goliath against themselves, but David measured the Philistine giant against the God he served and was able to face him boldly.

After they exchanged words and met each other on the battlefield, the true battle began: "Reaching into his bag and taking out a stone, he slung it and struck the Philistine on the forehead. The stone sank into his forehead and he fell down on the ground" (1 Samuel 17:49). Then the grand finale: "David ran and stood over him. He took hold of the Philistine's sword and drew it from the sheath. After he killed him, he cut off his head with the sword. When the Philistines saw that their hero was dead, they turned and ran" (1 Samuel 17:51). The Israeli army defeated the

Philistine army and "David took the Philistine's head and brought it to Jerusalem; he put the Philistine's weapon in his own tent" (1 Samuel 17:54).

What a victory it was as David boldly defeated Goliath, armed only with a slingshot and five smooth stones! The will of the Philistines was broken, and the Israelites were reinvigorated, all because a little shepherd boy answered the call of God. What are some key elements we can take away from this story on facing giants?

ONE – humility, obedience, and patience before the battle. David was in the field, minding his own business, doing his job, when he was sent to the battle by his father. Keep in mind David had already been anointed future king of Israel by Samuel (at the direction of God) but was still in the field working and taking direction from his father. He was where God wanted him in the field initially, despite being anointed king, and he answered the call to the battlefield to defend Israel, in God's name.

TWO – remember what God has already done for you. David recalled his victories over the lion and the bear, and he was able to face Goliath boldly. Despite his age and size disadvantage, David did not see them as disadvantages because he knew the Lord, the God of Israel, was with him.

THREE – attack your giant! We have to run into battle, not run from our giants, and use what God has given us. David showed faith and courage. He ran out quickly to meet his opponent, he did not hesitate, he did not negotiate, he ran into battle, and he attacked. God empowered him to use what was in his hand and he won with the weapons he was familiar with, trained with; not unfamiliar, unnecessary weapons.

FOUR – realize the battle belongs to the Lord. If we face giants in our own strength, we will lose. We must use a similar approach to David to face our own proverbial, figurative, or spiritual battles. We must lean on God, His strength and His power to overcome our giants. We cannot defeat our giants (problems, addictions, emotions, issues) on our own. We can't defeat our adversary, the Devil, and his evil spiritual forces in spiritual warfare without giving God the battle. We must use the Holy Spirit, Scripture, and the appropriate armor to win our battles (see Chapter 11 The Armor of God). If the battle is too big for us, then it is perfect for God. We must give the battle to the Lord. God took David through battles to prepare him to become king, and similarly, God takes us through battles to prepare us for our mission for the Kingdom of God.

GIANTS IN THE LAND

As they considered entering the land, weighing the risks and threats, Moses and the Israelites explored the land of Canaan, the Promised Land. "The Lord said to Moses, 'send some men to explore the land of Canaan, which I am giving to the Israelites. From each ancestral tribe send one of its leaders'" (Numbers 13:1-2). Moses sent them into the land and at the end of forty days they returned back to the Israelite camp. "They gave Moses this account: 'We went into the land to which you sent us, and it does flow with milk and honey! Here is its fruit. But the people who live there are powerful, and the cities are fortified and very large. We even saw descendants of Anak there'" (Numbers 13:27-28).

It appeared that the men were saying, "on one hand the land is great, filled with milk, honey, and fruit, however, on the other hand there are some significant, powerful enemies; some serious threats." "Then Caleb silenced the people before Moses and said, 'We should go up and take possession of the land, for we can certainly do it'" (Numbers 13:30). Despite the risks and adversity, Caleb was willing and ready to possess the land. The other spies who went in with Caleb countered with the following:

> "We can't attack those people; they are stronger than we are." And they spread among the Israelites a bad report about the land they had explored. They said, "The land we explored devours those living in it. All the people we saw there are of great size. We saw the Nephilim there (the descendants of Anak come from the Nephilim). We seemed like grasshoppers in our own eyes, and we looked the same to them."
>
> —NUMBERS 13:31-33

Caleb's counterparts, the other spies, outnumbered him and used false information, a "bad report," to convince Moses and the Israelites not to enter the Promised Land. They were dissuaded and afraid to step into what God had promised them. They were afraid of the giants (Nephilim) in the land and in verse 33: "We seemed like grasshoppers in our own eyes, and we looked the same to them." Comparatively to the giants they felt like grasshoppers. Although, the giants never actually saw the Israelites, the spies assumed they would look the same to them, like grasshoppers.

Their giants didn't physically stop them from entering the land, but their own thoughts, fears, and perceptions did. They created their own *giants* in their mind. Their thoughts became their giants, their opposition, and their failure. Caleb and Joshua were ready to enter and were leaning on their faith in God, and His promises. The other ten spies were not ready and were leaning on fear. They altered the fate of an entire generation of Israel who never entered the Promised Land and died in the wilderness, with the exception of Caleb and Joshua. Several years later, Joshua led the new generation of Israelites across the Jordan River and into the land that God had promised them.

If the Israelites under Moses' leadership would have compared the giants to God, as opposed to comparing their giants to themselves, they may have had the courage to take the land. We can learn from this as well. We should compare our giants (our problems, addictions, issues, threats, etc.) to God, not to ourselves. When a problem becomes too big for us to handle, then we have to give that problem to God. The battle is the Lord's. The only way to defeat our giants is in God's strength, not our strength. Then, and only then, are we be able to step into the promises He has for us, our promised land.

GIANT ENEMIES

As we explore our "giants," lets revisit our three spiritual enemies: the world, the flesh, and the Devil. The first spiritual enemy is the *world*. The world is the literal world and the people around us, typically referring to unbelievers, and popular culture that is set up against God. The Apostle John warned against loving the world: "Do not love the world or anything in the world. If anyone loves the world, love for the Father is not in them" (1 John 2:15). He went on to define three temptations in the world: "For everything in the world—the lust of the flesh, the lust of the eyes, and the pride of life—comes not from the Father but from the world. The world and its desires pass away, but whoever does the will of God lives forever" (1 John 2:16-17).

It is important to understand these three temptations of the world and stand firm against them, fighting for holiness, and the Kingdom of God. "For though we live in the world, we do not wage war as the world does. The weapons we fight with are not the weapons of the world. On the contrary, they have divine power to demolish strongholds" (2 Corinthians 10:3-4). We fight against the temptations of the world, strongholds, and addictions with our spiritual weapons.

With that said, John noted that God *loves* the world. He wrote: "For God so **loved** the world that he gave his one and only Son, that whoever believes in him shall not perish but have eternal life" (John 3:16). So how can we "avoid" the world, combat the temptations of the world, as stated above, and also "love" the world at the same time? Afterall, God loves the world and Jesus died for the world, and, at one point, before trusting in Christ, we, too, were part of the world and its carnality. When we are told *not* to love the world, the Bible is referring to the world's corrupt system, not people. We are to love people, but we cannot sacrifice for both God and the system of the world that is in rebellion against Him.

On this topic of love, John expounds in 1 John 4: "Dear friends, since God so loved us, we also ought to love one another" (1 John 4:11). "**God is love**. Whoever lives in love lives in God, and God in them" (1 John 4:16) and "we love because he first loved us" (1 John 4:19). John was saying we ought to love others, including believers and non-believers alike. We cannot conform to the ways of the world. We have to say "no" to the temptation of sin, to the ways of the world, but then still love the people of the world, showing them the love of Christ. It is attainable by developing "spiritual boundaries" and by following the guidance of the Holy Spirit and God's Word.

When asked which is the greatest commandment: "Jesus replied: 'Love the Lord your God with all your heart and with all your soul and with all your mind.' This is the first and greatest commandment. And the second is like it: 'Love your neighbor as yourself'" (Matthew 22:37-39). Jesus made the distinction fairly simple - love God and love people. Although it can become very complex to love your neighbor and love people in our everyday lives and even in ministry, the directive is simple, to love. The Apostle Paul understood this and wrote: "And now these three remain: **faith, hope, and love**. But the greatest of these is **love**" (1 Corinthians 13:13).

The second spiritual enemy is the *flesh*. In his letter to the Romans, Paul was saying this second enemy comes from within. Paul said he does what he doesn't want to do because of following the desires of his flesh. We are the same way, battling the desires of the flesh. Having conflict inwardly is normal for all, even Christians following God. Scripture says that we are born sinners and that we are by nature sinners. Our flesh is our enemy. Paul goes on to say, "what a wretched man I am! Who will rescue me from this body that is subject to death? Thanks be to God, who delivers me through Jesus Christ out Lord" (Romans 7:24-25)! Thankfully we can overcome sin, our flesh, and death because of Jesus. Jesus overcame death and we are not subject to the law, though the law is important to understand, as it helps us to recognize our sinful nature and our need for a Savior.

Further regarding the flesh, Paul wrote: "The mind governed by the flesh is hostile to God; it does not submit to God's law, nor can it do so. Those who are in the realm of the flesh cannot please God" (Romans 8:7-8). The flesh is against God and at odds with the Holy Spirit. Paul goes on to differentiate the flesh and the Spirit: "You, however, are not in the realm of the flesh but are in the realm of the Spirit, if indeed the Spirit of God lives in you. And if anyone does not have the Spirit of Christ, they do not belong to Christ" (Romans 8:9).

We see further direction on this with the letter to the Galatians regarding the fruit of the Spirit. In this letter Paul talks more about the flesh and the Spirit being at odds with each other and encourages us to walk by the Spirit. "So, I say, **walk by the Spirit**, and you will not gratify the desires of the flesh" (Galatians 5:16). It is by the Holy Spirit that we are able to lead a Christian life. The Spirit puts in us a new heart which trusts God and follows His ways. Ezekiel says, "**a new heart** I will give you and a new spirit I will put within you…I will put my Spirit within you and cause you to walk in my statutes" (Ezekiel 36:26-27 ESV). The life we have in Christ is given wholly to the work of the Spirit, who helps us battle against the desires of our flesh. Paul goes on to give us a comprehensive list of acts of the flesh to avoid (see Galatians 5:19-21). Contrast that with the fruit of the Spirit: "But the fruit of the Spirit is love, joy, peace, forbearance, kindness, goodness, faithfulness, gentleness and self-control" (Galatians 5:22-23).

The third and final spiritual enemy is the *Devil*. The word "Devil" comes from the Greek word "Diablos" and it means slanderer or false accuser. The Bible refers to the Devil as the "accuser of our brothers and sisters" (Revelation 12:10), "the father of lies" (John 8:44), "the god of this age" (2 Corinthians 4:4), and "the prince of this world" (John 14:30). As discussed in the opening chapter of this book, Satan comes only to "steal, kill, and destroy" (John 10:10). Peter warned us: "Be alert and of sober mind. **Your enemy the devil** prowls around like a roaring lion looking for someone to devour. Resist him, standing firm in the faith, because you know that the family of believers throughout the world is undergoing the same kind of sufferings" (1 Peter 5:8-9). The Devil is our enemy and prowls around like a roaring lion, looking to devour. Peter says to be alert, of sober mind, resist him, stand firm, and remember that other believers are going through similar battles around the world.

Regarding resisting the Devil, James wrote: "Submit yourselves, then, to God. Resist the devil, and he will flee from you. Come near to God and he will come near to you" (James 4:7-8). We must submit to God and resist the Devil and he will flee. Regarding standing firm in the faith, this is addressed further in Ephesians 6 with the "Armor of God" (see Chapter 11 Armor of God). John wrote: "You, dear children, are from God and have overcome them, because the one who is in you is greater than the one who is in the world" (1 John 4:4). Greater is He who is in us; by the power of Jesus, the Holy Spirit, and the Word of God, we can overcome the Devil. We cannot defeat him on our own accord. Remember: "We are able to triumph over him by the blood of the lamb and the word of our testimony" (see Revelation 12:11).

CHAPTER EIGHT

STORMS

*Peace I leave with you; my peace I give you. I
do not give to you as the world gives. Do not let
your hearts be troubled and do not be afraid.*

—JOHN 14:27

We have all been through storms in our lives – literal, physical storms. Some have been through tornadoes, hurricanes, flooding, earthquakes, and more. Therefore, this topic of storms is a relatively easy concept to identify with when we talk in terms of spiritual storms or spiritual warfare. Storms can come on quickly and cause severe damage in our lives. Others may take time to build and hang around for a period of time, drenching us with rain and floods. Whichever the case, we know that these storms can cause ferocious, life-changing, and long-lasting damage that must be dealt with. We also know that we can prepare for physical storms before they come and can also recover and rebuild after they are gone. We can apply these same concepts to "spiritual storms." In this chapter we will look at "spiritual storms" in the context of fear, foundation, focus, and faith.

FEAR – A TALE OF TWO STORMS

In Mark 4, we see the tale of the *first storm*. While on a boat ride on the Sea of Galilee, Jesus was sleeping, and a storm arose. As the storm nearly swamped the boat, the disciples were afraid and woke Jesus up. "He got up, rebuked the wind and said to the waves, 'Quiet! Be Still!' Then the wind died down and it was completely calm. He said to the disciples, 'Why are you so afraid? Do you still have no faith'" (Mark 4:39-40)? The language of this verse strongly suggests that this storm may have been caused by demonic activity, maybe even to drown Jesus. And the disciples, who were experienced boatmen, were afraid, despite Jesus being in the boat with them. They had already witnessed Jesus perform miracles, but they believed that the storm was more powerful than Jesus and acted accordingly – in a panic! They did not acknowledge, or believe, that Jesus ruled over the powerful storm. In fact, when Jesus woke up, they cried out, "Teacher, do you not care that we are perishing" (Mark 4:38 NKJV)? Surely, you and I would have been calm and trusted Jesus in the storm, right?

In Mark 6 we see the tale of the *second storm*. This time Jesus was not in the boat. He sent the disciples out on the lake, while He went up on a mountainside to pray. He was apparently watching them from a distance as "he saw the disciples straining at the oars, because the wind was against them. Shortly before dawn he went out to them, walking on the lake" (Mark 6:48). When they first saw Him, they thought He was a ghost and were afraid, "immediately he spoke to them and said, 'Take courage! It is I. Don't be afraid.' Then he climbed into the boat with them, and the wind died down. They were completely amazed" (Mark 6:50-51).

As we compare the tale of two storms, we see that Jesus was in the boat with them in the first storm, but He was away from them, yet nearby, during the second storm. Also, we see that during the first storm Jesus was asleep, whereas during the second storm, He was awake praying. Just before the second storm, the disciples witnessed Him perform a miracle, the feeding of the 5,000. During both storms the disciples were afraid, including when Jesus walked out on the water, they thought He was a ghost. Fear was a very real emotion for them in these stories, as it is with us, especially while battling the storms of life.

Jesus was testing and building their faith. He gave them a revelation of who He is and that He has control over the natural, physical, and spiritual realms, if they would just trust Him. I believe He is trying to teach us the same. We must allow Jesus to ask us the same question that He asked His disciples: "Why are you so afraid? Have you still no faith" (Mark 4:40 ESV)? We must recognize that if the natural world and the supernatural world obeyed Him, what else would be impossible to Him?

I also have a theory that since they saw Him calm the first storm in Mark 4, perhaps He wanted to see if they would have the faith to try and calm the second storm in Mark 6. Afterall, He showed them how to calm the first storm previously. Maybe He was praying to the Father in Heaven for them while He was on the mountainside. If only they would have the faith to ditch fear, calm the storm, and to rebuke demonic forces just as He had! But unbelief dominated them again. Remember the story in

Mark 17, about the young boy who suffered with seizures? The disciples had failed to cast out a demon from the boy because of their unbelief. Faith activates power. Faith can move mountains and it can also rebuke storms.

Matthew's account takes the story one step further: Jesus had Peter step out of the boat and walk on the water with Him, testing his faith further (see Matthew 14). Sometimes Jesus asks us to step out in faith with Him as well, encouraging us to keep our eyes fixed on Him alone, despite the raging storm around us.

As we learn to navigate "spiritual storms" in our own lives, we must grow to learn that true peace is not the absence of the storm, it is finding *peace* in the storm. Paul encouraged Timothy with this: "For God has not given us a spirit of fear, but of power and of love and of a sound mind" (2 Timothy 1:7 NKJV). After telling them to not be anxious about anything, but pray in every situation, Paul told the Philippians: "And **the peace of God**, which transcends all understanding, will guard your hearts and your minds in Christ Jesus" (Philippians 4:6-7). We can learn from the disciples in both storms and from these other Scriptures. Peace has a name and His name is Jesus! We can invite Jesus into our boats during a storm. We can find peace in the storm, lean on the Holy Spirit, pray about everything, and let the peace of God guard our hearts and minds in Christ Jesus.

FIRM FOUNDATION

We know that "spiritual storms" are inevitable. They will come eventually and sometimes often; we must be prepared with a *firm* foundation. This leads us to the story Jesus told of the "wise builder":

> Therefore, everyone who hears these words of mine and puts them into practice is like a wise man who built his house on the rock. The rain came down, the streams rose, and the winds blew and beat against that house; yet it did not fall, because it had its foundation on the rock. But everyone who hears these words of mine and does not put them into practice is like a foolish man who built his house on sand. The rain came down, the streams rose, and the winds blew and beat against that house, and it fell with a great crash.
>
> —MATTHEW 7:24-27

Jesus used this parable to explain the importance of a firm foundation. Of course, He was using this as symbolism as to what to build their figurative or spiritual house on and, really, their life on. He was saying build your life on the *rock*, not the sand. Building your life on the rock will ensure stability when the storms come. Again, not *if*, but *when* the storms come. We must be ready for the storms and build our lives on Jesus, the solid rock of our salvation. Psalms 46 says, "God is our refuge and strength, an ever-present help in trouble. Therefore, we will not fear, though the earth gives way and the mountains fall into the heart of the sea" (Psalms 46:1-2). God is our refuge and our strength in our time of trouble.

As we take this one step further, Jesus exclaimed to Peter that it was on the rock that He planned to build His Church. Jesus asked His disciples in Matthew's Gospel, "who do people say the Son of Man is?' They replied, 'some say John the Baptist; others say Elijah; and still others, Jeremiah or one of the prophets'" (Matthew 16:13-14). "Simon Peter answered, 'You are the Messiah, the Son of the living God'" (Matthew 16:16). Then Jesus replied:

> Blessed are you, Simon son of Jonah, for this was not revealed to you by flesh and blood, but by my Father in Heaven. And I tell you that you are Peter, and **on this rock I will build my church**, and the gates of Hades will not overcome it. I will give you the keys of the kingdom of heaven; whatever you bind on earth will be bound in heaven, and whatever you loose on earth will be loosed in heaven.
>
> —MATTHEW 16:17-19

Jesus told Peter that his answer and understanding of who He is, was a revelation from heaven. Sometimes we need a *revelation* from heaven. We need God to reveal something supernatural to us; we need God to reveal Himself to us. We also need to understand who we think Jesus is and who He is to us personally, as individuals. This is a fundamental and life-changing, eternity-changing question, that we all must come to terms with and answer. If Jesus is not your personal Savior, then I pray you make Him so! If you need a revelation from heaven, then I pray you reach out to God and search His Scripture and that He may reveal Himself to you in a tangible way.

Often, we need God to show up and reveal Himself in a specific season or storm; to show us a way out. In the passage above, Jesus addressed Simon as Peter or *Petros*, which means *rock* and told Peter that he would be the one to establish His church. Jesus changed Simon's name after he was the first to publicly confess Jesus as Messiah and Son of the living God. This is something God did often in the Bible, such as changing Abram to Abraham, Saul to Paul. Sometimes He will change our names, too; we keep our birth names, but prophetically God will call us by a different name. This is the absolute authority of God. He calls us *children* of God, co-heirs with Christ, His righteousness through Christ! We have to begin to believe it and speak it over ourselves. Despite Peter's failures, Jesus told him that he would be the anchor of the Church.

Jesus went on further to explain that the gates of Hades (Hell) will not overcome the Church. Satan and Hell cannot overcome the Church of Jesus Christ. This is an important concept in spiritual warfare! If you are in a battle or storm, then come together with the Church. Reach out for prayer and stand with the Church. Jesus also explained to Peter that whatever he binds on earth, it will be bound in heaven and vice versa; a yes on earth is a yes in heaven and vice versa. This reminds me of the "Lord's Prayer" and Jesus teaching the disciples:

> This, then, is how you should pray: "Our Father in heaven, hallowed be your name, your kingdom come, your will be done, on earth as it is in heaven. Give us today our daily bread. And forgive us our debts, as we also have forgiven our debtors. And lead us not into temptation but deliver us from the evil one."
>
> —MATTHEW 6:9-13

In the "Lord's Prayer," Jesus was teaching the disciples and us about the importance of starting prayer with reverence to God: "Hallowed be your name" (honor to God and His holy name). He says, "your kingdom come, your will be done, on earth as it is in heaven." He is teaching about the "Kingdom of God" manifesting on earth and in our lives. He is also teaching about prayer for supplication (needs), forgiveness, delivery from temptations, and delivery from "the evil one." This prayer highlights the invitation for the Kingdom of Heaven to manifest on earth and to overcome Satan. If we want to win in spiritual warfare, then we must understand this prayer and how to pray, and we must pray often.

To survive the storms of life, we must have our foundation on the rock, Jesus. We must join together and lean on the Church of Jesus Christ. We need to lean on the Kingdom of God, here on earth. In our times of trouble, we can come to God in prayer. He will fight for us and we will win in His name, by faith, and for His glory. We can become what Isaiah calls "oaks of righteousness": "They will be called oaks of righteousness, a planting of the Lord for the display of splendor" (Isaiah 61:3).

FOCUS IN THE STORM

In the storms of life, during spiritual warfare, it is easy to lose focus. The storm rages around us, the enemy distracts us, there is wind, rain, debris, and all kinds of obstacles. We focus on things that don't truly matter and lose focus on what matters most. It is easy to do. Our first instinct is often to panic as the disciples did or lean on default responses or people that we have established as fail safes in our own strength, rather than pray and lean on God or our local churches and prayer partners.

We may have low visibility in the natural, but if we choose, then we can seek visibility in the spiritual. Paul wrote to the Ephesians:

> I keep asking that the God of our Lord Jesus Christ, the glorious Father, may give you the Spirit of wisdom and revelation, so that you may know him better. I pray that the **eyes of your heart may be enlightened** in order that you may know the hope to which he has called you, the riches of his glorious inheritance in his holy people.
>
> —EPHESIANS 1:17-18

Paul was praying that the "eyes of their heart" would be opened to see. He was praying for them and encouraging them to get a revelation, to see in the spiritual realm, not just the natural. We have to see in the natural and move in the natural, take steps of faith, if you will, but we must learn to see and understand in the spiritual as well. That way in the storms, when things are often low visibility in the natural, we can learn to navigate in the spiritual realm, leaning on God, trusting that He has power over the wind and the waves. The writer of Proverbs put it this way: "Trust in the Lord with all your heart and lean not on your own understanding; in all your ways submit to him, and he will make your paths straight" (Proverbs 3:5-6). Trust in the Lord. Submit to Him. He will guide your steps. Psalms 119:105 exclaims: "Your word is a lamp for my feet, a light on my path."

How do we fine tune our spiritual vision or our spiritual eyes? Mark records a story about a blind man healed by Jesus, that might illuminate this concept for us:

> When he had spit on the man's eyes and put his hands on him, Jesus asked, "Do you see anything?" He looked up and said, "I see people; they look like trees walking around." Once more Jesus put his hands on the man's eyes. Then his eyes were opened, his sight was restored, and he saw everything clearly. Jesus sent him home, saying, "Don't even go into the village."
>
> —MARK 8:23-26

With the first touch or the first pass the man's vision improved some and he saw people "that looked like trees walking around." It wasn't so clear at first. With the second touch or second pass the man's sight "was restored and he saw everything clearly." We see that his sight was restored and so he must not have always been blind, as we see that he knew what trees and people looked like. He needed a second touch by Jesus to restore his sight. Many preachers will say it wasn't the power of Jesus at fault here, but the man's faith. He needed a second touch so that his faith could level up to the healing power and will of Jesus for his life. This man's literal sight was restored, his faith revealed and so it is with us and our spiritual sight and "spiritual eyes."

We can learn from this story. Similar to what Paul is trying to teach us in Ephesians 1 above, we need to open the eyes of our heart and get a spiritual revelation or vision of what God is trying to do in our lives. This will happen when we level up our faith to God's power, authority, and will for our lives. We can get a vision for His mission for our lives in the spiritual realm and allow it to guide our ambitions and goals and manifest in the natural. We will get a second touch and truly see His plan for our lives and utilize this tool or ability, in faith, over and over going forward. God encourages us: "Call to me and I will answer you and tell you great and unsearchable things you do not know" (Jeremiah 33:3).

As we begin to see in the spiritual realm and get a progressive revelation of who God is and how to operate in this realm, we can begin to fix our focus in the middle of the storm. Paul wrote: "So, we **fix our eyes** not on what is seen, but on what is unseen, since what is seen is temporary, but what is unseen is eternal" (2 Corinthians 4:18). He was encouraging us to fix our eyes on the eternal, not just the temporary life at present. To have a heavenly, eternal focus in the storm. Again, the writer of Hebrews encourages us to: "**Fix our eyes** on Jesus, the pioneer and perfecter of faith" (Hebrews 12:2). Keep our eyes on salvation, eternity, and Jesus. Remember, He is the one who calms the storms and gives us strength in the storm.

FAITH IN THE STORM

This brings us to the story of Paul caught in the middle of a storm. Paul was a prisoner on his way to Rome for potential trial by Caesar. Before setting sail, Paul warned them, "men, I can see that our voyage is going to be disastrous and bring great loss to ship and cargo, and to our own lives also" (Acts 27:10). But the centurion did not listen to

Paul's advice, and they set out for sail. Paul wrote: "Before very long, a wind of hurricane force, called the Northeaster, swept down from the island. The ship was caught by the storm and could not head into the wind; so, we gave way to it and were driven along" (Acts 27:14-15). Now in a hurricane type storm they were driven along, at will to the force of the storm, the plot thickened, and the danger built.

In a relatively elaborate and intense fashion, Paul went on in Acts 27 to explain the "violent battering" they took, how the "storm continued raging," and "we finally gave up all hope." After several days Paul reminds them, they should have taken his advice not to sail, nonetheless, he shared a revelation that he had received from God:

> Last night an angel of the God to whom I belong and whom I serve stood beside me and said, "Do not be afraid, Paul. You must stand trial before Caesar; and God has graciously given you the lives of all who sail with you." So, keep up your courage, men, for I have faith in God that it will happen just as he told me. Nevertheless, we must run aground on some island.
>
> —ACTS 27:23-26

Run aground on some island indeed they did. We learn in Acts 28 that they landed on the island of Malta and all the men on the ship survived. Paul received a revelation from God that He had a plan for Paul to stand before Caesar and, therefore, would not die in this storm. This promise, however, was not a new one. Two years earlier, Jesus himself stood by Paul in prison and promised: "As you have testified to the facts of me in Jerusalem, so you must also testify in Rome" (Acts 23:11). Yet, sometimes in the midst of a terrifying storm, we need to be reminded of the promise God has already given. Paul then knew without a doubt that they would not die in the storm and he encouraged the rest of the crew with the assurance of that promise. Despite their miscalculations and not listening to Paul, God still spared them. But now they were shipwrecked on an island.

On the Island of Malta, in Acts 28, we see that Paul was bitten by a snake and survived. Again, God spared Paul's life because he was still on a mission from God. He was shown kindness by the inhabitants of the island and later brought to the home of the chief official of the island. We see that: "His father was sick in bed, suffering from fever and dysentery. Paul went in to see him and, after prayer, placed his hands on him and healed him. When this had happened, the rest of the sick on the island came and were cured" (Acts 28:8-9). Paul was on a mission, an assignment from God to get to Rome, but in the meantime was shipwrecked on Malta and healed every sick person on the island.

After this shipwrecked time on Malta, Paul finally sailed for Rome. He wrote: "They honored us in many ways; and when we were ready to sail, they furnished us with the supplies we needed. After three months we put out to sea in a ship that had wintered in the island" (Acts 28:10-11). He was there for three months, but what was the purpose? Perhaps the shipwreck was just due to their folly and this was just a coincidence. Or perhaps it was a part of God's plan all along, to have Paul heal and minister to these people, to share the Gospel. Or perhaps it was spiritual warfare; Satan thought he could shipwreck Paul and kill him or have a snake bite him and kill him, but he failed. What Satan meant for evil, God used for good. We may never know which of these scenarios are correct, but either way, Paul got a revelation from God, went on mission on the island, and then went onto his mission in Rome.

We can learn from Paul in this storm in Acts 27 and his time on Malta in Acts 28. The storm can come at us for many different reasons. It could be from fault of our own, part of God's plan or Satan trying to thwart us. Maybe God lets it pass through His own hands to us for a greater purpose. No matter the reason, we should look for revelations from God. We should look for His purposes in the storm and after the storm. God might be revealing His presence in our life or trying to fix our focus or assign us a new mission for His Kingdom.

We should certainly celebrate when we make it to the other side of the storm. However, true faith manifests when we celebrate in the storm or at least stand on faith in God in the middle of the storm. We must take heart in the storm, as David wrote: "I would have lost heart, unless I had believed That I would see the goodness of the LORD In the land of the living" (Psalms 27:13 NKJV). We need to get a promise, prophecy, or word from God in the middle of the storm. Then we stand on that promise or word for the breakthrough during the trial. We triumph when we focus on Jesus and see through to the other side of the storm. We prophesy the promise and we stand on it until we see it come to pass. These are the building blocks of true faith and how to withstand spiritual warfare and spiritual storms.

PART 3

SPIRITUAL VICTORY

CHAPTER NINE

PRODIGAL

*I have been crucified with Christ and I no
longer live, but Christ lives in me. The life I
now live in the body, I live by faith in the Son
of God, who loved me and gave himself for me.*

—GALATIANS 2:20

The word prodigal means "one who spends or gives lavishly
and foolishly" or "one who has returned after an absence."[1]
The most well-known and applicable story of this in the
Bible is the Apostle Luke's account of the "Prodigal Son."
There is a lot for us to learn from this story about stewardship,
relationships, and ultimately about God as our Father and us
as His children. We can then subsequently apply this story
to repentance, salvation, God's protection, and ultimately
overcoming spiritual warfare and obtaining spiritual victory!

THE PRODIGAL SON

The story of the "Prodigal Son" was told by Jesus to a Jewish
audience as "The Parable of the Lost Son." Jesus used

symbolism that the audience would have been familiar with to relate to them, to drive His points home, and ultimately encourage them to repentance and relationship with God. The parable started with the story of a man with two sons: "And the younger one said to the father, 'Father, give me my share of the estate.' So, he divided his property between them" (Luke 15:12). This was not the custom for sons to get their inheritance early in life, so immediately in the story the audience would have realized something was awry.

"Not long after that, the younger son got together all he had, set off for a distant country and there squandered his wealth in wild living" (Luke 15:13). Hence, the title "prodigal" applied to this young man. He ran away from home, forgot the values he had been taught, blew his inheritance on parties and fleshly desires, and now there was a famine in the country he was staying. He had to resort to working for a man who "sent him to his fields to feed his pigs" (Luke 15:15). He was so hungry that he began to consider eating the pigs' food. Mind you, this was a young Jewish man and they did not eat pork or associate with pigs and they certainly did not eat pigs' food. At this point the audience hearing this story would no doubt have been enthralled and disgusted at the same time.

At this low point in his life, at rock bottom, this young man had an epiphany – it was time to go home. He realized his father may not restore him to his previous position in the family dynamic or hierarchy, but even if his father made him a servant, at least he would have food. He planned to say to him, "Father, I have sinned against heaven and against you. I am no longer worthy to be called your son; make me like one of your hired servants" (Luke 15:18-19).

So, he headed towards his father's house and the following scene ensued:

> But while he was still a long way off, his father saw him and was filled with compassion for him; he ran to his son, threw his arms around him and kissed him. The son said to him, "Father, I have sinned against heaven and against you. I am no longer worthy to be called your son." But the father said to his servants, "Quick! Bring the best robe and put it on him. Put a ring on his finger and sandals on his feet. Bring the fattened calf and kill it. Let's have a feast and celebrate. For this son of mine was dead and is alive again; he was lost and is found." So, they began to celebrate.
>
> —LUKE 15:20-24

While he was still a long way off, the father *ran* to him. This was not a custom for the men in this culture to run anywhere and certainly not to a son that had shamed the family; a son who took his inheritance, left home, and squandered it. A son who disrespected his family and everything that their Jewish culture and customs stood for. But the father didn't care about custom or anything the prodigal son had done. Instead, he ran to him! Why? Because if the village elders had gotten to him first, they would have held a "ceremony of shame" known in Hebrew as Kezazah, which literally means to "cut off."[2] They would have chastised him and told him he was no longer welcome. So, the father had to meet him first with grace before the elders could meet him with the law. The father welcomed him with open arms, with a different ceremony in mind, a homecoming party to celebrate the return of his son.

The prodigal son was okay with being a servant, yet he was restored to his previous position in the household and with celebration, magnificence, and pomp. We see in verse 21 that "the son said to him, 'Father, I have sinned against heaven and against you. I am no longer worthy to be called your son.'" The son came home with a repentant attitude and heart. He knew that he had sinned against his father, he admitted that, and he turned from his ways. We can deduce that he was asking for forgiveness, and the father loved him and restored him. This, Jesus tells us, is what God is like. The "Prodigal Son" was for the audience then and for us today to see a display of the love and grace of our Heavenly Father to those who repent and turn to Him.

Paul wrote this to the church at Corinth: "Godly sorrow brings repentance that leads to salvation and leaves no regret, but worldly sorrow brings death" (2 Corinthians 7:10). Worldly sorrow is simply just saying, "I'm sorry I got caught or messed up." Godly sorrow is true, humble repentance of our transgressions against God; saying, "God I messed up, I now have changed my ways, I turn away from them completely, please forgive me, and help me stop." Paul was saying that Godly sorrow and repentance leads to salvation and helps us live without regret and move on from our past.

SALVATION AND REDEDICATION

On the topic of salvation, Paul in his letter to the Romans wrote: "For all have sinned and fall short of the glory of God" (Romans 3:23) but "God demonstrates his own love for us in this: While we were still sinners, Christ died for us" (Romans 5:8). Paul went on to write: "For the wages of sin is death, but the gift of God is eternal life in Christ Jesus our Lord" (Romans 6:23). We are all sinners. We all need to repent. God loves us and has shown us His mercy and grace, similar to the Prodigal Son, by covering our sinfulness in the robe of Christ's righteousness. Despite our sin, *Christ died for us*. He takes away our sins so that we may have a relationship with God and spend eternity with Him. But we have to be willing to humble ourselves and repent of our sins and subsequently accept this salvation and enter into that relationship with Him.

A little further on this topic - how do we enter into this relationship with God and accept the salvation of Jesus? Paul answers that for us and wrote: "If you declare with your mouth, 'Jesus is Lord,' and believe in your heart that God raised him from the dead, you will be saved. For it is with your heart that you believe and are justified, and it is with your mouth that you profess your faith and are saved" (Romans 10:9-10). Paul says, we have to believe in our hearts that God raised Jesus from the dead and we have to declare it with our mouth. In other words, we have to say it out loud that we believe this, and we will be saved. "For, everyone who calls on the name of the Lord will be saved" (Romans 10:13). Just like previous chapters in this book, we've discussed believing and speaking things out, praying to God the Father for things to manifest.

We confess this faith with a prayer similar to this one, by saying: "Dear Lord Jesus, I know that I am a sinner, and I ask for your forgiveness. I believe you died for my sins and rose from the dead. I turn from my sins and invite

You to come into my heart and life. I want to trust and follow you as my Lord and Savior."

This prayer is commonly referred to in churches and other arenas as "the sinner's prayer." Essentially, the purpose is praying to God, putting your faith in Jesus, meaning it, and you will be saved. You will come into right relationship with and trust God, through Jesus Christ by faith. Paul wrote: "For it is by grace you have been saved, through faith, it is a gift of God – not by works, so that no one can boast" (Ephesians 2:8-9). We are not saved by works, but by God's grace which is His gift to us, through faith in Jesus Christ. The Bible calls us to do works, such as written in the Book of James. James was not preaching a different gospel path to salvation, but he was saying that true faith will reveal itself in good works. Also, I want to add, it is not about religion, but about a true and intimate relationship with Jesus Christ.

"Therefore, if anyone is in Christ, the new creation has come: The old has gone, the new is here" (2 Corinthians 5:17)! When we become saved, we become "a new creation"; we turn from our old ways and live for God now and spend eternity with Him. One key point, as mentioned above, is that salvation comes after true repentance, turning from our ways, and living for God. I also encourage you to connect with a local church for further guidance on this topic of salvation and further teaching and understanding of God's Word and to have fellowship with other believers. This is very important!

I am not a pastor, and, therefore, meeting with a pastor and coming under their teaching and leadership is essential. If you have said this prayer, then tell them you have accepted Jesus Christ as your Lord and Savior and ask them to guide you further in prayer and teaching. Make sure you understand salvation completely, even after reading about it here. Perhaps some of you are doing a "rededication." Similar to the Prodigal Son, you had a relationship with the Father, you are returning back to Him, and through Christ you are rededicating your life to Him. I commend you on your decision and congratulate you!

David wrote: "Create in me a pure heart, O God, and renew a steadfast spirit within me. Do not cast me from your presence or take your Holy Spirit from me. Restore to me the joy of your salvation and grant me a willing spirit, to sustain me" (Psalms 51:10-12). Return to God and He will return to you. He will create in you a pure heart and grant you the Holy Spirit, and bring you joy. Return to God and let Him restore you. Jesus said, "come to me, all you who are weary and burdened, and I will give you rest. Take my yoke upon you and learn from me, for I am gentle and humble in heart, and you will find rest for your souls. For my yoke is easy and my burden is light" (Matthew 11:28-30).

Do not delay in your decision to turn to God or turn back to God. *This is your moment!* You may not have another moment. I can't see your future or my future, but the opportunity is now! Perhaps the Holy Spirit is drawing you in to pray. In his letter, James wrote: "Why, you do not even know what will happen tomorrow. What is your life? You are a mist that appears for a little while and then vanishes" (James 4:14). Our life is but a mist. We don't know what tomorrow holds. We have the opportunity to spend eternity in Heaven with God. We also have the opportunity to spend our lives now serving Him, living for Jesus, and loving people. Ephesians 2 went on to say, "for we are God's handiwork, created in Christ Jesus to do good works, which God prepared in advance for us to do" (Ephesians 2:10). We can go on to do works that God has prepared for us to do and live for Him. What an honor!

BECOMING DISCIPLES

Jesus encouraged us to live for Him daily and it will benefit our self (our souls):

> Then he said to them all: "Whoever wants to be my disciple must deny themselves and **take up their cross** daily and **follow me**. For whoever wants to save their life will lose it, but whoever loses their life for me will save it. What good is it for someone to gain the whole world, and yet lose or forfeit their very self?"
>
> —LUKE 9:23-25

We have to learn to become Jesus' disciples and, therefore, "pick up our crosses daily," our assignments, our missions, and diligently follow Him. Disciple comes from the word discipline. We have to learn to "lose our life for His sake" or give up our plans for His plans, our desires for His desires, our personal kingdoms for His Kingdom. In serving Him, however, we don't lose our souls to the world. Instead, we gain our "true selves," develop our "true souls," and we gain everything through Christ, by faith.

The prophet Isaiah wrote: "'For my thoughts are not your thoughts, neither are your ways my ways,' declares the

Lord. 'As the heavens are higher than the earth, so are my ways higher than your ways and my thoughts than your thoughts'" (Isaiah 55:8-9). Jesus said, "but seek first his kingdom and his righteousness, and all these things will be given to you as well" (Matthew 6:33). God has our best interests in mind. He will give us all we need if we live for Him and seek Him. Paul wrote: "Now to him who is able to do immeasurably more than all we ask or imagine, according to his power that is at work within us, to him be glory in the church and in Christ Jesus throughout all generations, for ever and ever! Amen" (Ephesians 3:20-21).

CHILDREN OF GOD

When we come into relationship with God, He is our Heavenly Father and we are His children. Paul wrote: "Because you are his sons, God sent the Spirit of his Son into our hearts, the Spirit who calls out, 'Abba, Father.' So, you are no longer a slave, but God's child; and since you are his child, God has made you also an heir" (Galatians 4:6-7). He also wrote: "The Spirit you received does not make you slaves, so that you live in fear again; rather, the Spirit you received brought about your adoption to sonship. And by him we cry, 'Abba, Father'" (Romans 8:15). Paul was telling these churches and us that we are children of God through the Spirit and through adoption. We can cry out to Him as our Father. We are no longer slaves to sin, but God's children. What a revelation and a promise!

Paul in that same passage in Romans wrote: "Now if we are children, then we are heirs-heirs of God and co-heirs with Christ, if indeed we share in his sufferings in order that we may also share in his glory" (Romans 8:17). We become God's adopted children and co-heirs with Christ. It doesn't matter what names the world or others call you; it only matters what God calls you. And God calls you *His child.* That holds more weight and more power than anything anyone else can try to label you. To see God as your loving Father, though, may not come easily if you carry the scars of a bad relationship with your earthly father. But we have to recognize that our father-image is flawed and in no way fits an accurate picture of our heavenly Father; even the best earthly father is a blurred representation of our heavenly Father. Like a good father, God has anticipated your every need and provided for it (See Matthew 6:25-34). He loves you! And "if God is for us, who can be against us" (Romans 8:31)?

GOD'S LOVE AND PROTECTION

So, what does this all mean for spiritual warfare? Salvation or rededication to Jesus is the most important decision of your life. Understanding God's will and promise in our lives also means we gain God's love and protection. God's love and protection means victory in spiritual warfare! On this topic, Romans 8 ends like this:

> No, in all things we are more than conquerors through him who loved us. For I am convinced that neither death nor life, neither angels nor demons, neither the present nor the future, nor any powers, neither height nor depth, nor anything else in all creation, will be able to separate us from the love of God that is in Christ Jesus our Lord.
>
> —ROMANS 8:37-39

If we are not in relationship with God, living for Jesus, living under God's protection, then we are fully subject to Satan, his schemes, and his dark spiritual forces. When we live for God, we are His children, and we fall under His umbrella, hedging, and protection. Paul was saying *nothing* can separate us from the love of God that is in Christ Jesus. We also have access to His Word, the Holy Spirit, and every other opportunity and weapon afforded to us from Him.

CHAPTER TEN

THE BATTLE WITHIN

You will keep in perfect peace those whose
minds are steadfast, because they trust in you.
—ISAIAH 26:3

God designed us as complex beings made up of mind (soul, psyche, emotions), body, and spirit, that are distinct entities, but interact with each other in concert at any given moment. Paul wrote: "May your whole spirit, soul, and body be kept blameless at the coming of our Lord Jesus Christ" (1 Thessalonians 5:23 NLT). Not only do we face spiritual battles, as we have looked at in length, but we have battles in our own minds and emotions. I refer to the battle in the mind as *"the battle within."* We will look at Scripture that deals with warfare of the mind, guarding the mind, renewing the mind, and how that relates to relationships and other aspects of our daily lives.

WARFARE OF THE MIND

Not all thoughts come from God. Some come from the enemy. As we explored previously, we have three enemies - the world, the flesh, and the Devil. Paul wrote: "The mind governed by the flesh is hostile to God; it does not submit to God's law, nor can it do so. Those who are in the realm of the flesh cannot please God" (Romans 8:7-8). The mind governed by the flesh and the world will lead us to trouble and out of fellowship with God. Additionally, the Devil and his evil forces will try to put thoughts in our minds. His goal is to entice us to sin and separate us from God. He uses distraction, deception, and any mode necessary to negatively affect our minds.

In the battlefield of spiritual warfare, where does the mind fit on the chessboard or in the game of life? Is the mind the pawn, rook, knight, queen, or even the king of the game? Surely the mind is the king of spiritual warfare, right? It is none of these. The mind is the entire chessboard! In the chess game of life or in spiritual warfare, the mind is the battlefield where war is waged. Of course, the spirit and body are engaged in the battle as well, but the mind is a significant stage for battle.

As we discussed previously, the Devil is an accuser, liar, slanderer, and tries to separate us from God. The Devil will even try to get us to question our salvation. The Bible tells us to "put on the helmet of salvation" (see Ephesians 6:17). We put on the helmet to spiritually protect our minds and to hold onto our understanding that we are indeed saved. Our minds will always be a battlefield, but we are not a slave to the mind. We instead have the power to demolish strongholds, arguments, and every pretension that comes against us and the knowledge of God. Paul wrote to the Corinthians:

> The weapons we fight with are not the weapons of the world. On the contrary, they have divine power to demolish strongholds. We demolish arguments and every pretension that sets itself up against the knowledge of God, and we take captive every thought to make it obedient to Christ.
>
> —2 CORINTHIANS 10:4-5

Strongholds are lies that contradict the power and person of Jesus. Strongholds are addictions or issues in our lives that can try to enslave us. Strongholds will try to build a fortress in our minds. They can go from a small campfire (stronghold) to a large forest fire (fortress) quickly that can have devastating consequences in our minds and in our spiritual lives. But the passage above says we have the power to overcome the strongholds and other things that come against us. We can overcome the lies and strongholds with the Word and the power of Christ. We must watch our thoughts, take captive every thought and submit it to Christ, because they can become words, habits, character, and can affect our very future.

GUARD THE MIND

Take heart! Often when the Bible refers to the heart, it is referring to the mind and emotions. Proverbs says: "For as he thinks in his heart, so is he" (Proverbs 23:7 NKJV). The

Bible also tells us to guard our hearts and minds. "Above all else, guard your heart, for everything you do flows from it" (Proverbs 4:23). God will help us guard our minds through Jesus if we let Him: "And the peace of God, which transcends all understanding, will guard your hearts and your minds in Christ Jesus" (Philippians 4:7). Let the Holy Spirit and manifestation of the fruit of the Spirit help us to overcome the battle for the mind as well.

We must also develop a keen sense of discernment and wisdom through the Word and the guidance of the Holy Spirit. Paul wrote to the Corinthians: "But I am afraid that just as Eve was deceived by the serpent's cunning, your minds may somehow be led astray from your sincere and pure devotion to Christ" (2 Corinthians 11:3). He is warning us not to be deceived or let the deceiver get in our minds. Stay devoted to Christ. In this passage he also warned against false gospels and false practices. Proverbs encourages us to "trust in the LORD with all your heart, and do not lean on your own understanding. In all your ways acknowledge him, and he will make straight your paths" (Proverbs 3:5-6 ESV) and "many are the plans in a person's heart, but it is the Lord's purpose that prevails" (Proverbs 19:21). We must lean on God to guide us and allow His purposes to prevail in our hearts, all the while staying focused as to not be led astray.

There is an exceptional amount of teaching on "wisdom" throughout the Bible. We gain wisdom by God's Word and by walking with Him. The Psalmist wrote: "Your word is a lamp for my feet, a light on my path" (Psalms 119:105). Regarding wisdom, James wrote: "If any of you lacks wisdom, you should ask God, who gives generously to all without finding fault, and it will be given to you" (James 1:5). Later he wrote: "You do not have because you do not ask" (James 4:2 NKJV). James encouraged us to seek God for wisdom and to ask Him for guidance. Discernment, wisdom, and guarding the heart and mind are crucial in winning the battle of the mind.

RENEW THE MIND

After receiving salvation by grace, through faith in Jesus, and becoming a child of God, our spirit is new, and we become a new creation in Christ. However, we still have the same mind as we had before we were saved. We have to *renew* the mind. Paul wrote to the Romans: "Do not conform to the pattern of this world but be transformed by the renewing of your mind. Then you will be able to test and approve what God's will is—his good, pleasing and perfect will" (Romans 12:2). We have to restructure the mind, our thinking, and the activities that we do. We can't think or live as the world does. Rather, we have to allow God's Word and the Holy Spirit to renew our minds daily. We have to take on the mind of Christ. Paul wrote: "Who has known the mind of the Lord as to instruct him? But we have the mind of Christ" (1 Corinthians 2:16).

When asked what the greatest commandment is, "Jesus replied: 'Love the Lord your God with all your heart and with all your soul and with all your mind.' This is the first and greatest commandment. And the second is like it: 'Love your neighbor as yourself'" (Matthew 22:37-39). He instructed us to love God with all of our heart, soul, and *mind*. We are to engage our minds in love for God and people. The prophet Jeremiah wrote: "You will seek me and find me when you seek me with all your heart" (Jeremiah 29:13) and "call to me and I will answer you and tell you great and unsearchable things you do not know" (Jeremiah 33:3). God encourages us to seek Him and call to Him and we will find Him, and He promises to tell us great and unsearchable things. We seek Him not only with our spirit, but also with our mind and He responds not only to our spirit, but also to our mind, things that we "do not know."

RELATIONSHIP MINDSET

In the battle for the mind, the Devil would love nothing more than to destroy our marriages, families, and friendships. If he can destroy relationships, then he can isolate us and try to destroy our destinies in the Kingdom of God. How do we combat the enemy in our relationships directly? In our relationships, Paul encouraged us to have the same mindset of Christ:

> In your relationships with one another, have the same **mindset as Christ Jesus**: Who, being in very nature God, did not consider equality with God something to be used to his own advantage; rather, he made himself nothing by taking the very nature of a servant, being made in human likeness. And being found in appearance as a man, he humbled himself by becoming obedient to death— even death on a cross!
>
> —PHILIPPIANS 2:5-8

Paul encouraged us to follow Christ's example of humility and servant to all, displayed during His ministry here on earth. He was the ultimate sacrifice with His death on the Cross for your sins, my sins, and the sins of all mankind for all eternity. We are not instructed to die on a cross, but to "pick up our cross daily and follow Him" (see Luke 9:23). We are to treat each other as Christ would want us to and to think with *His mindset*.

By God's grace, perhaps we can enter into true fellowship with each other, as did the believers of the early Church in Acts. Luke wrote: "They devoted themselves to the apostles' teaching and to fellowship, to the breaking of bread and to prayer" (Acts 2:42). May we have the same devotion! The Apostle Paul wrote to the church at Corinth: "For when we came into Macedonia, we had no rest, but we were harassed at every turn—conflicts on the outside, fears within. But God, who comforts the downcast, comforted us by the coming of Titus" (2 Corinthians 7:5-6). Paul was writing about his persecution while on mission and the fact that he was comforted by Titus, a fellow believer, a brother in the faith. We, too, have the opportunity and ability to comfort each other in times of persecution and spiritual warfare as well. May we be encouragers, seeking fellowship with one another, and may we help each other pick up our mantles and fight the good fight of faith.

Paul wrote to the Ephesians regarding the relationship between husbands and wives and encouraged spouses to "submit to one another out of reverence for Christ" (Ephesians 5:21). He went on to say, "wives, submit yourselves to your own husbands as you do to the Lord" (Ephesians 5:22) and "husbands, love your wives, just as Christ loved the church and gave himself up for her" (Ephesians 5:25). Submission here means to yield out of respect; it is a natural expression of humility. To respect and love. It is not a subjugation, it is not forced, but an act of free will. He was encouraging husbands and wives to love and respect each other. In all of our relationships, we must take on the *mindset of Christ*, operate in humility, pick up our crosses daily, and love and respect each other. Then not only can we follow God's commands, but we can beat the Devil in the battle of our minds and live fuller, richer lives.

Another extremely important concept regarding relationships and overcoming the enemy is forgiveness. Forgiveness takes a weapon out of Satan's hands and opens the door for God to work in a situation. Paul wrote to the church in Ephesus: "Do not let the sun go down while you are still angry, and do not give the devil a foothold" (Ephesians 4:26-27). John wrote this about forgiveness from God: "If we confess our sins, he is faithful and just and will forgive us our sins and purify us from all unrighteousness" (1 John 1:9).

What does the Bible say about forgiving each other? It says that forgiveness is paramount: "For if you forgive other people when they sin against you, your heavenly Father will also forgive you" (Matthew 6:14). But how often should we forgive? One and done, right? "Then Peter came to Jesus and asked, 'Lord, how many times shall I forgive my brother or sister who sins against me? Up to seven times?' Jesus answered, 'I tell you, not seven times, but seventy times seven'" (Matthew 18:21-22). Jesus was saying that we must forgive each other over and over again. This can be very challenging and sometimes we have to forgive from a distance (set up boundaries), especially if safety is an issue, but we must learn to forgive, nonetheless. When we forgive others it then sets us free; it frees our minds from bitterness and can release healing in our hearts, lives, and relationships.

PSYCHE AND EMOTIONS

Psychological and psychiatric conditions can be a very real, multifaceted, and complex phenomena. Anxiety, depression, insomnia, and hundreds of other conditions can alter and even cripple our lives. Do not hesitate to seek care from a physician, psychologist, or counselor. Medication, counseling, and other modalities of treatment can be very helpful for chemical imbalances of the brain and improper ways of operating or thinking. With that said, some of the disorders of the mind, alterations in psyche, and imbalances in emotions can have a spiritual component as well.

The enemy would love nothing more than for you to be distracted, dysfunctional, and deceived. However, Christ wants you to be healed, whole, and effective. Isaiah wrote about Jesus coming to die for our sins and also to heal our wounds - mind, body, and spirit. "But he was pierced for our transgressions, he was crushed for our iniquities; the punishment that brought us peace was on him, and by his wounds we are healed" (Isaiah 53:5). He took on our *sin* so we could be saved. He took on our *wounds* so that we could be healed. We can invite Christ into the deep places of our heart and give Him our emotions, psyche, and conditions and He will heal us. Then we can hopefully say, "it is well with my soul."

When we invite Christ to heal our mind, body, and spirit then we can be made well. We can beat the Devil in the battle of the mind. David wrote: "The Lord is my shepherd, I lack nothing. He makes me lie down in green pastures, he leads me beside quiet waters, he refreshes my soul" (Psalms 23:1-3). Jesus said, "I am the good shepherd. The good shepherd lays down his life for the sheep" (John 10:11). He also said, "Come to me, all you who are weary and burdened, and I will give you rest. Take my yoke upon you and learn from me, for I am gentle and humble in heart, and you will find rest for your souls. For my yoke is easy and my burden is light" (Matthew 11:28-30). Jesus is our good Shepherd; He will give us rest and refresh our souls, if we come to Him, if we let Him.

SANCTIFICATION

I mentioned part of this passage at the beginning of this chapter but wanted to expound on it regarding sanctification. Paul wrote: "May God himself, the God of peace, sanctify you through and through. May your whole spirit, soul and body be kept blameless at the coming of our Lord Jesus Christ. The one who calls you is faithful, and he will do it" (1 Thessalonians 5:23-24). Paul encouraged us to keep our mind, body, and spirit blameless, and he explains that God will help us with this. He is faithful. He will sanctify us. Sanctification means, "to make holy, set apart as sacred, or to consecrate."[1] Remember what Joshua told the Israelites prior to crossing over the Jordan River into the Promised Land. "Consecrate yourselves, for tomorrow the Lord will do amazing things among you" (Joshua 3:5).

The Bible takes sanctification and consecration very seriously and so should we. For help in explaining this topic, I will quote Pastor Jentezen Franklin: "Sanctification is the process of becoming holy in daily life; it is practicing purity and being set apart from the world and from sin. Sanctification is allowing the Holy Spirit to make us more like Jesus in what we do, in what we think, and in what we desire."[2] He went on later to add: "Sanctification is the key to being in God's will."[2] On this topic, Paul wrote: "For this is the will of God, your sanctification" (1 Thessalonians 4:3 NKJV). Although, complex topics to navigate, sanctification and consecration are important for us to understand and engage in for the battle of the mind and for victory in spiritual warfare.

CHAPTER ELEVEN

THE ARMOR OF GOD

The night is nearly over; the day is almost
here. So let us put aside the deeds of darkness
and put on the armor of light.

—ROMANS 13:12

Hopefully this book has helped you to better understand that we are engaged in spiritual warfare at its finest, and it is a *fight* for our souls. We are warriors, engaged in a war! The prophet Joel wrote: "Proclaim this among the nations: Prepare for war! Rouse the warriors! Let all the fighting men draw near and attack" (Joel 3:9). Paul wrote to the church at Corinth: "For though we live in the world, we do not wage war as the world does. The weapons we fight with are not the weapons of the world. On the contrary, they have divine power to demolish strongholds" (2 Corinthians 10:3-4). What are these weapons we fight with that have divine power? How do we prepare for this battle and survive the spiritual war?

THE ARMOR OF GOD

In his letter to the church at Ephesus, Paul wrote about the concept of "The Armor of God." Paul began his teaching: "Finally, be strong in the Lord and in his mighty power. Put on the full armor of God, so that you can take your stand against the devil's schemes" (Ephesians 6:10-11). Paul started by saying be strong in the Lord and His power; receive strength from the Lord. Jesus made it clear to His disciples where their spiritual authority and power came from: "All authority in heaven and on earth has been given to me" (Matthew 28:18) and "I have given you authority to trample on snakes and scorpions and to overcome all the power of the enemy; nothing will harm you" (Luke 10:19). As stated in a previous chapter, we cannot defeat the Devil in our own power, but we can defeat him with the power and authority given to us by Jesus.

So then why put on the armor of God? Paul was saying so that we can "take our stand against the devil's schemes." He wrote: "For our struggle is not against flesh and blood, but against the rulers, against the authorities, against the powers of this dark world and against the spiritual forces of evil in the heavenly realms" (Ephesians 6:12). This is spiritual warfare and we, therefore, need spiritual armor and weapons of warfare. We are fighting against these evil powers of the world and heavenly realms, and also against the Devil's evil schemes. So, what are his evil schemes exactly?

As discussed previously, the word "Devil" comes from the Greek word "Diablos" and it means "slanderer" or "false accuser." The Bible refers to the Devil as the "accuser of our brothers and sisters" (Revelation 12:10) and "the father of lies" (John 8:44). His schemes are, therefore, false accusations and lies. We are in a *war of words*, and we must be ready for them to come against us. The Devil is our enemy and prowls around like a roaring lion looking for someone to devour (see 1 Peter 5:8-9). In other words, he is looking for a spiritual battle at any time or in any season. The false accuser speaks into our circumstances to lie, accuse, disrupt, persecute, and separate us from God. He will try to get in our minds about our faith, relationships, career, finances, health, and any area he can.

It is for these reasons that Paul wrote: "Therefore, put on the full armor of God, so that when the day of evil comes, you may be able to stand your ground, and after you have done everything, to stand. Stand firm" (Ephesians 6:13-14). We are not preparing for *if* the day of evil comes, but *when*. Our day of evil may not just be one season, but several different seasons throughout our lives. Another version put it this way: "Be prepared. You're up against far more than you can handle on your own. Take all the help you can get, every weapon God has issued, so that when it's all over but the shouting you'll still be on your feet" (Ephesians 6:13-14 MSG).

Paul then went on in this passage to lay out "The Armor of God" in detail:

> Stand firm then, with the belt of truth buckled around your waist, with the breastplate of righteousness in place, and with your feet fitted with the readiness that comes from the gospel of peace. In addition to all this, take up the shield of faith, with which you can extinguish all

the flaming arrows of the evil one. Take the helmet of salvation and the sword of the Spirit, which is the word of God.

—EPHESIANS 6:14-17

In this passage, Paul was using armor fitted for a Roman soldier, which was the ruling power during this time period. He did this to give a visual correlation to spiritual weapons. To give examples in the natural or physical realm to help us understand and apply them to the spiritual realm and spiritual warfare. The message version put it this way: "Truth, righteousness, peace, faith, and salvation are more than words. Learn how to apply them. You'll need them throughout your life" (Ephesians 6:14-17 MSG).

Many of the pieces in the armor are *defensive*, such as the breastplate, helmet, and shield. The breastplate of righteousness protects our heart. Wear it and do right things by the power of the Holy Spirit. When we do this the Devil is frustrated and put back. Paul was saying that righteousness, salvation, and faith are all protective measures. The helmet over our heads helps us to remember our salvation and its power through Jesus; the enemy can't take away our salvation. Knowing this protects us from the Devil's mind games. The shield of faith will extinguish all the flaming arrows (accusations, lies, attacks) of the evil one. Hold it tightly in every attack! The belt of truth holds the armor all together and is thus a subsequent staple in our defense against the enemy. The feet fitted with the readiness that comes from the Gospel of peace – this footwear makes us ready for battle and there is peace through Christ in the process.

In contrast to the defensive weapons above, an *offensive* weapon in our spiritual arsenal is the sword of the Spirit, which is the Word of God. Use of the Word, or tactical use of Scripture, can be very powerful in spiritual warfare. Fight lies with God's truth! Just as Jesus defeated the Devil by using Scripture in the wilderness in Matthew 4, so can we. The writer of Hebrews wrote: "For the word of God is alive and active. Sharper than any double-edged sword, it penetrates even to dividing soul and spirit, joints and marrow; it judges the thoughts and attitudes of the heart" (Hebrews 4:12). The prophet Isaiah wrote: "So is my word that goes out from my mouth: It will not return to me empty but will accomplish what I desire and achieve the purpose for which I sent it" (Isaiah 55:11). God encouraged Joshua, "keep this Book of the Law always on your lips; meditate on it day and night, so that you may be careful to do everything written in it. Then you will be prosperous and successful" (Joshua 1:8).

One important key with Scripture as a weapon - it must be spoken out loud by us against the enemy. Here it refers to the Rhema Word or the spoken Word of God. We must read the Word, understand it, but then speak it into action! Remember in Revelation 12, John called the Devil the "accuser of our brothers and sisters" (see Revelation 12:10). He then wrote: "They triumphed over him by the blood of the lamb and the word of their testimony" (Revelation 12:11). They used their words (testimony) to overcome the Devil and so should we! Our testimony is about the blood of the lamb and through Him we are strengthened, forgiven, redeemed, and we can overcome the enemy. We go in Christ's strength through us, we utilize the power and authority of His name, we use the words of our testimony, and we speak God's Word. While in the fight, we must get a Scripture or several Scriptures, stand on them (stand firm), speak them, and fight back!

THE WEAPON OF PRAYER

After Paul described the formal makeup of the armor of God in Ephesians 6, he then wrote: "And pray in the Spirit on all occasions with all kinds of prayers and requests" (Ephesians 6:18). Some consider prayer or praying in the Spirit to be an additional offensive weapon and relate it to the Roman spear or javelin, which could be thrown a decently far distance in battle. To the Corinthians, Paul wrote: "So what shall I do? I will pray with my spirit, but I will also pray with my understanding; I will sing with my spirit, but I will also sing with my understanding" (1 Corinthians 14:15). We pray to God and praise Him, with singing, with our understanding or in our "usual fashion," but we also pray and praise with our spirit.

In his letter to the Romans, Paul explains further what it means to "pray in the Spirit":

> In the same way, the Spirit helps us in our weakness. We do not know what we ought to pray for, but the Spirit himself intercedes for us through wordless groans. And he who searches our hearts knows the mind of the Spirit, because the Spirit intercedes for God's people in accordance with the will of God.
>
> —ROMANS 8:26-27

To sum up this concept, prayer is a weapon, especially when combined with Scripture, the sword of the Spirit. So, at our disposal, we have the offensive weapons of spear and sword. "God's Word is an indispensable weapon. In the same way, prayer is essential in this ongoing warfare. Pray hard and long" (Ephesians 6:17-18 MSG). Paul was saying even when we don't know what to pray, the Holy Spirit intercedes for us; He prays on our behalf! To top this off, lest we forget, "Christ Jesus who died – more than that, who was raised to life – is at the right hand of God and is also interceding for us" (Romans 8:34). We, therefore, have the Holy Spirit and Jesus interceding for us. What a powerful concept! We must put on the full armor of God to win in spiritual warfare!

The last part of Ephesians 6:18 says, "with this in mind, be alert and always keep on praying for all the Lord's people." We must throw the javelin or spear at the enemy not just for ourselves, but for our brothers and sisters in Christ. Always be alert and always pray! In his letter to the church at Thessalonica, Paul wrote: "Rejoice always, pray continually, give thanks in all circumstances, for this is God's will for you in Christ Jesus" (1 Thessalonians 5:16-18). The NKJV says, "pray without ceasing!"

PRAISE BEFORE BREAKTHROUGH

On the concept of praying on all occasions and using prayer as a weapon, I'm reminded of the story of Paul and Silas in prison in the Book of Acts. It all started when Paul and Silas were being followed by a "female slave who had a spirit by which she predicted the future.

She earned a great deal of money for her owners by fortune-telling" (Acts 16:16). Paul became so annoyed with her following and shouting at them for many days that "he turned around and said to the spirit, 'in the name of Jesus Christ I command you to come out of her!' At that moment the spirit left her" (Acts16:18). The slave girl's owners became angry, since they lost their ability to make money off of her, and they riled up the local people and authorities. This led to Paul and Silas being beaten and thrown into prison. "The jailer was commanded to guard them carefully. When he received these orders, he put them in the inner cell and fastened their feet in the stocks" (Acts 16:23-24).

So, we see in this story that Paul and Silas were chained up in the "inner cell" or the innermost part of the prison, likely what resembled a dungeon, for their actions. Then the following happened:

> About midnight Paul and Silas were praying and singing hymns to God, and the other prisoners were listening to them. Suddenly there was such a violent earthquake that the foundations of the prison were shaken. At once all the prison doors flew open, and everyone's chains came loose. The jailer woke up, and when he saw the prison doors open, he drew his sword and was about to kill himself because he thought the prisoners had escaped. But Paul shouted, "Don't harm yourself! We are all here!" The jailer called for lights, rushed in and fell trembling before Paul and Silas. He then brought them out and asked, "Sirs, what must I do to be saved?" They replied, "Believe in the Lord Jesus, and you will be saved—you

and your household." Then they spoke the word of the Lord to him and to all the others in his house.

—ACTS 16:25-32

We see that while in the innermost cell of a dungeon, despite being beaten and shackled, awaiting their fate from the authorities, Paul and Silas began "praying and singing hymns to God." Likely most of us would have been in pain physically, scared mentally, and not focused on the spiritual realm. However, Paul and Silas knew how to "pray and give thanks in all circumstances" or "pray without ceasing" (1 Thessalonians 5:17 NKJV). They were singing and praising God before the answer came or before they knew the outcome. Undoubtedly, the other prisoners heard them praising and saw the whole scene unfold. Paul was looking to share the Gospel in all situations, even in chains. As a result, the jailer and his whole household heard the Gospel and were saved.

As we have seen, prayer is a weapon against the enemy and Paul and Silas used it and God delivered them. In his letter to the Ephesians, Paul wrote: "Be filled with the Spirit, speaking to one another with psalms, hymns, and songs from the Spirit. Sing and make music from your heart to the Lord, always giving thanks to God the Father for everything, in the name of our Lord Jesus Christ" (Ephesians 5:18-20). In Philippians he wrote: "Do not be anxious about anything, but in every situation, by prayer and petition, with thanksgiving, present your requests to God" (Philippians 4:6). He went on to explain in that passage: "I have learned the secret of being content in any and every situation" (Philippians 4:12) and "I can do all this through him who gives me strength" (Philippians 4:13).

Hopefully, we, too, can learn to be thankful, to pray in all circumstances and pray without ceasing; to praise God for who He is and what He has done in our lives, not just what we hope He will do. We can learn to take "praise breaks" throughout the day whether we are up or down, in a moment of heaviness or in times of joy. We can also learn the concept that often "praise precedes breakthrough" or we can learn to "praise before breakthrough." Jesus said to the woman at the well, "yet a time is coming and has now come when the true worshipers will worship the Father in the Spirit and in truth, for they are the kind of worshipers the Father seeks" (John 4:23). The Father is seeking true worshippers!

The Bible says that God is enthroned upon the praises of His people, or more specifically: "Yet you are holy, enthroned on the praises of Israel" (Psalms 22:3 ESV). This reminds me of King Jehoshaphat and the people of Israel who won a battle with praise and worship alone, while outnumbered by enemy armies three to one. In 2 Chronicles 20, through a prophet, God told Jehoshaphat and his army: "You will not have to fight this battle. Take up your positions; stand firm and see the deliverance the Lord will give you, Judah and Jerusalem. Jehoshaphat bowed down with his face to the ground, and all the people of Judah and Jerusalem fell down in worship before the Lord" (2 Chronicles 20:17-18). As the enemies approached, Jehoshaphat appointed men to sing to the Lord and to praise Him saying: "Give thanks to the Lord, for his love endures forever" (2 Chronicles 20:21). God won the battle for them against their enemies. We can learn to praise God in our battles as well. If the battle is too big for us, then it is perfect for God. Give the battle to the Lord and praise Him through the process.

We have to praise God prior to seeing the end of a trial or challenging season, before we see how it plays out. We can worship our way through the battles and learn to "worship through the worry." We can thank Him for the outcome, before it happens, although it is ultimately up to His will and timing in the end. Get a word from Scripture, pray it out loud over and over and believe for a miracle and for breakthrough; we can "prophesy the promise," all the while praising Him for who He is, even in the process. This is having faith in the middle of the battle, trial, or storm, and believing God will work out the details. When we praise God through any situation, we can begin to understand the truth of Nehemiah's words: "Do not be worried, for the joy of the LORD is your strength and your stronghold" (Nehemiah 8:10 AMP).

GARMENT OF PRAISE

On the day that I was about to finish writing this chapter of the book, specifically regarding prayer and praise, I decided to go and pray at one of the local churches. As I was walking into the prayer room, one of the church workers, whom I had never met, stopped me and asked how I was doing and what I was there to pray for? I told her I was there to pray for *breakthrough*. She told me that she had a word from the Lord directly for me. She encouraged me to cast off the "spirit of heaviness" (despair) and put on a "garment of praise." Isaiah wrote: "To console those who mourn in Zion, to give them beauty for ashes, The oil of joy for mourning, The **garment of praise** for the **spirit of heaviness**" (Isaiah 61:3 NKJV).

During our conversation, she went on to give me a word about remembering that we are seated with Christ in the heavenly places. She quoted: "And God raised us up with Christ and seated us with him in the heavenly realms in Christ Jesus" (Ephesians 2:6). I believe she gave me a word of wisdom or word of knowledge. If you are interested, see 1 Corinthians 12:8 for more information on the spiritual gifts of providing a message of wisdom or message of knowledge.

While talking to the woman at the church, I looked over and saw a painting on the wall nearby. It was a picture of what appeared to be a father praying over a sleeping child, while angels were engaged in spiritual warfare in the background scene. I had walked by this painting on my way to the prayer room several times before and never noticed it. This time I couldn't help but notice it and the inscription written below it. I approached it and read, in small letters at the bottom of the painting: "*Spiritual Warfare*" and "Ephesians 6:12."[1] Not only is spiritual warfare the main concept of this book, but Ephesians 6:12 is one of the central verses and it was already included in this chapter. As I went on my way, I was encouraged that God had a word for me and I was standing on that word and began praising Him before the breakthrough.

CHAPTER TWELVE

VICTORY

For everyone born of God overcomes the
world. This is the victory that has overcome
the world, even our faith.
—1 JOHN 5:4

Throughout the book we have looked at what spiritual battles and spiritual warfare are and how to overcome the enemy on the battlefield. Ultimately, we want to establish victory in spiritual warfare and, as we have discussed, we do that through Jesus Christ, the Holy Spirit, and the weapons of our warfare. My goal in this last chapter is to summarize some key concepts from the book and give "7 keys to spiritual victory."

1 | PROBLEMS

The first key to spiritual victory in spiritual warfare is to have *problems*. That is to have victory itself, we must, there-fore, have battles or actual problems in our life. In other words, there can't be a victory without a battle. If you are in spiritual warfare, that means the enemy is opposing you and trying to stop your purpose for the Kingdom of God. If you never experience spiritual warfare, then perhaps you are going the same direction as the enemy or even playing on the same team.

When we go through adversity and trials, we must identify the problems and attack them. We must identify the enemies, which we have seen are the world, the flesh, and the Devil. Also, we must identify the giants in our lives - those things that come against us in opposition, such as addictions, habits, or personal characteristics that we want to overcome or change. We must strengthen our faith in the face of giants or while in the midst of the fires or storms of life. We will be victorious, by the grace and strength God gives us. We will learn that what the enemy meant for evil God will use for good. What the people intended to use to harm us, God will use to help strengthen us. He will help us not only survive, but thrive, and He will get the glory.

2 | PERSON

The second key to spiritual victory in spiritual warfare is to have a *person* with us in the battle. But not just any person; we need the person of Jesus Christ! Victory and hope have a name and His name is Jesus! Because of Jesus and His victory on the Cross, we don't battle *for* victory, but *from* victory. In his letter to the Corinthians, Paul wrote: "But thanks be to God! He gives us the **victory** through our Lord Jesus Christ" (1 Corinthians 15:57). To the Colossians, Paul wrote: "He canceled the record of the charges against us and took it away by nailing it to the cross. In this way, he disarmed the spiritual rulers and authorities. He shamed them publicly by his **victory** over them on the cross" (Colossians 2:14-15 NLT).

I encourage you to speak victory over your life in every battle or situation, even before you see the victory. Again, this is instituting the approach of "prophesy your promise" and "praise before your breakthrough." Thank Him for the victory, before you even see the outcome. We must get a word from His Word and we must stand on it. We must compare every lie from the enemy and every stronghold against the Word of God. We don't know exactly how each battle will go, but the war has already been won by Jesus, so step up for battle! Tell yourself, "I'm going to see a victory!" Pray the "resurrection life and glory of Jesus" over your situation.

Remember, Christ in you, *the hope of glory.* Paul wrote about this to the Colossians: "To them God has chosen to make known among the Gentiles the glorious riches of the mystery, which is Christ in you, the hope of glory" (Colossians 1:27). We have hope and peace in Jesus and in the personhood of the Holy Spirit as well! Paul wrote to the Romans: "May the God of **hope** fill you with all joy and **peace** as you trust in him, so that you may overflow with **hope** by the power of the Holy Spirit" (Romans 15:13).

Understanding Jesus' ministry can help us understand who He is and what we should do in our own lives and ministries. Jesus came to earth, fully man and fully God, to die on the Cross for our sins, but also for so much more. While reading from Isaiah 61, Jesus proclaimed: "The Spirit of the Lord is on me, because he has anointed me to proclaim good news to the poor. He has sent me to proclaim freedom for the prisoners and recovery of sight for the blind, to set the oppressed free, to proclaim the year of the Lord's favor" (Luke 4:18-19). Later in His ministry, Jesus also said, "the blind receive sight, the lame walk, those who have leprosy are cleansed, the deaf hear, the dead are raised, and the good news is proclaimed to the poor" (Luke 7:22). Therefore, we can see that Jesus came to save, preach, teach, heal, set the captives free, serve the poor and needy, and raise the dead! We must ask ourselves who do we think Jesus is? Who is He to us personally, and what does that mean for our lives? As we begin to understand these fundamental questions, it will shape our focus and future, and we can have spiritual victory!

3 | PURPOSE/PLAN

The third key to spiritual victory in spiritual warfare is to discover and understand God's *purpose and plan* for our lives. We must seek God and establish our identity in Christ. Not identity in the world, position, power, money, or anything else, but in Jesus Christ alone. In the beginning of this book we looked at Jesus' purpose and plan for our lives, compared to Satan's. Jesus said, "the thief comes only to steal and kill and destroy; I have come that they may have life and have it to the full" (John 10:10). Another version says, "life abundant." Christ wants us to have an abundant life through Him. Paul wrote: "God is able to bless you abundantly, so that in all things at all times, having all that you need, you will abound in every good work" (2 Corinthians 9:8). He wants to bless us so we can bless others. We are saved from sin, but also saved for a life of *purpose*.

David wrote: "You prepare a table before me in the presence of my enemies. You anoint my head with oil; my cup overflows. Surely your goodness and love will follow me all the days of my life, and I will dwell in the house of the Lord forever" (Psalms 23:5-6) and "I would have lost heart, unless I had believed that I would see the goodness of the LORD In the land of the living" (Psalms 27:13 NKJV). David knew of God's goodness and His purpose and he knew, despite his battles, despite his enemies, God would deliver him. I want to present a few more Scriptures regarding God's purpose for us. Jeremiah wrote: "'For I know the plans I have for you,' declares the Lord, 'plans to prosper you and not to harm you, plans to give you hope and a future'" (Jeremiah 29:11). Proverbs says, "many are the plans in a person's heart, but it is the Lord's purpose that prevails" (Proverbs 19:21). Also, like Joshua, we must resolve and declare: "As for me and my household, we will serve the Lord" (Joshua 24:15). We must discover and understand God's plan and purpose for our lives.

Paul wrote: "Being confident of this, that he who began a good work in you will carry it on to completion until the day of Christ Jesus" (Philippians 1:6). Despite the season you are in or the spiritual battle you are enduring, God has a plan and a purpose for your life, and He will carry it on to completion, through Jesus. In that same chapter, Paul wrote: "For to me, to live is Christ and to die is gain" (Philippians 1:21). Paul was in prison and was prepared to die and see Jesus in heaven, but in the meantime, he knew God had a plan for him, and he knew to live is Christ. Do we have the same mindset? To live *is* Christ or to live *for* Christ - that is victory! Like Paul, we must also press on, in persistence for what God has for us: "Forgetting what is behind and straining toward what is ahead, I **press on** toward the goal to win the prize for which God has called me heavenward in Christ Jesus" (Philippians 3:13-14).

Christ died on the Cross to redeem us, to save us for eternity, but He also desires to work on us while we are here on earth, through a process called "restoration." This is similar to the concept of sanctification, discussed in a previous chapter. Paul wrote: "And we know that in all things God works for the good of those who love him, who have been called according to his purpose" (Romans 8:28). He wrote immediately after this: "For those God foreknew he also predestined to be conformed to the image of his Son, that he might be the firstborn among many brothers and sisters" (Romans 8:29). I believe what Paul was saying here is that we have been called for a *purpose*, to be conformed to the Image of His Son. We were made "in His image" (see Genesis 1:27), but that was disrupted with the fall of Adam and Eve in the garden. Jesus overcame the fall of man on the Cross; He redeemed us through His blood. Through our struggles and our hardships, we are now being restored to His Image, slowly becoming more like Christ. We are becoming sanctified and restored, during our lives here on earth. That is part of our purpose and His plan for us as the children of God, and during that process, He is working for our good.

4 | PREPARATION/PROTECTION

The fourth key to spiritual victory in spiritual warfare is to *prepare and protect* ourselves in spiritual battle. We reviewed at length the armor of God in Chapter 11. We are to put on the "full armor of God" daily to withstand the attacks from the enemy in spiritual warfare. We are to have courage and to stand as warriors in battle! Jim Cymbala wrote: "If we are courageous enough to go on the spiritual attack, to be mighty men and women of prayer and faith, there is no limit to what God can accomplish through us."[1] We previously reviewed the Scripture that says, "the Devil prowls around like a roaring lion" (1 Peter 5:8). Notice it says, the Devil is "like a lion." But our God *is a lion*; the Lion of Judah! We must also be as bold as lions ourselves. Proverbs says, "the wicked flee though no one pursues, but the righteous are as **bold as a lion**" (Proverbs 28:1). Paul wrote: "God made him who had no sin to be sin for us, so that in him we might become the righteousness of God" (2 Corinthians 5:21). We become righteous in God, through Jesus. We become bold as lions against the enemy, the roaring lion, through Jesus.

Proverbs says that God protects the righteous: "Surely, Lord, you bless the righteous; you surround them with your favor as with a shield" (Psalms 5:12). Proverbs also says, "the horse is made ready for the day of battle, but victory rests with the Lord" (Proverbs 21:31). Even though the victory is with the Lord, we must still prepare for the battle. Remember our authority and power come from Jesus and the victory rests with Him. "For the Lord your God is the one who goes with you to fight for you against your enemies to give you victory" (Deuteronomy 20:4). Isaiah wrote: "No weapon forged against you will prevail, and you will refute every tongue that accuses you. This is the heritage of the servants of the Lord, and this is their vindication from me,' declares the Lord" (Isaiah 54:17).

The Bible also talks at length about God being our *strength*. Isaiah wrote: "But those who hope in the Lord will renew their strength. They will soar on wings like eagles; they will run and not grow weary; they will walk and not be faint" (Isaiah 40:31). Psalms 46 says, "God is our refuge and strength, an ever-present help in trouble. Therefore, we will not fear, though the earth gives way and the mountains fall into the heart of the sea" (Psalms 46:1-2). Proverbs says, "the name of the Lord is a fortified tower; the righteous run to it and are safe" (Proverbs 18:10). The writer of Hebrews talked about angelic protection: "Are not all angels ministering spirits sent to serve those who will inherit salvation" (Hebrews 1:14)?

Lastly, I am reminded of Joshua, when God tells him, "have I not commanded you? Be strong and courageous. Do not be afraid; do not be discouraged, for the Lord your God will be with you wherever you go" (Joshua 1:9). Paul wrote to the Romans: "If God is for us, who can be against us" (Romans 8:31) and "nothing will be able to separate us from the love of God that is in Christ Jesus our Lord" (see Romans 8:39). To the Ephesians he wrote: "I pray that out of his glorious riches he may strengthen you with power through his Spirit in your inner being, so that Christ may dwell in your hearts through faith" (Ephesians 3:16). We must prepare and protect ourselves in spiritual warfare and the Lord will protect us as well. In Christ we go from strength to strength, glory to glory, and faith to faith.

5 | PRAYER/PRAISE/PERSISTENCE

The fifth key to spiritual victory in spiritual warfare is *prayer, praise, and persistence* in spiritual battle. The writer of Hebrews encouraged us how to approach God's throne room in prayer: "Let us then approach God's throne of grace with confidence, so that we may receive mercy and find grace to help us in our time of need" (Hebrews 4:16). Prayer and praise are integral parts in our worship of God. We can worship in a prayer service, worship in a "praise and worship" service, and also in our daily lives. Remember Paul said to "pray without ceasing" (1 Thessalonians 5:17 NKJV). Prayer and praise in a specific personal or group worship setting can be truly amazing, however Paul encouraged us to have prayer and praise every day, all day, without ceasing. Jesus told us, "but when you pray, go into your room, close the door and pray to your Father, who is unseen. Then your Father, who sees what is done in secret, will reward you" (Matthew 6:6). Enter the *secret place* and allow God to enter the middle of your circumstances and help you win the battle!

In a previous chapter we talked about the importance of listening for a word from God or getting a word in His Holy Word, and then speaking that word forth. Our power and authority come when we speak the name of Jesus and when we speak the Word of God over our lives. We talked about the concept of "hear the word, speak the word, then look for it, and you will see it," in both the "Valleys" and "Mountains" chapters. For example: Ezekiel in the "valley of dry bones" and Elijah on Mount Carmel. We looked at the persistence and repetition of Elijah in prayer, and how

God rewarded his persistence. We looked at the concepts of "praise before breakthrough" and "speaking those things that are not as though they were" (see Romans 4:17). We talked about "worshipping through worry" and "speaking life" over our own lives, even in the face of the enemy; even when things look bleak.

We looked at the concept of prayer and fasting at length, such as the story of Daniel, and how God rewarded his persistence, repetition, and fasting. We can also pray for breakthrough, especially through prayer and fasting. We can stand on God's Word and "believe that we receive it." We can "thank God before it happens." In the end, however, we will rely on His will and His timing, not our own. "Give thanks to the Lord, for he is good; his love endures forever" (1 Chronicles 16:34). "Be joyful in hope, patient in affliction, faithful in prayer" (Romans 12:12). Also, when we pray for each other it can be profoundly effective. James wrote: "Therefore, confess your sins to each other and pray for each other so that you may be healed. The prayer of a righteous person is powerful and effective" (James 5:16). Proverbs says, "as iron sharpens iron, so one person sharpens another" (Proverbs 27:17).

Previously, we discussed: "The most powerful avenue of prayer is when you say, 'Father I come in the name of Jesus and I plead the blood of the lamb.'"[2] I've heard many pastors over the years say to "pray what you read and hear in God's word." The practice of praying Scripture back to God can be very effective because you know you are praying His will and aligning with His Word. For example, we can pray this Scripture: "And my God will meet all your needs according to the riches of his glory in Christ

Jesus" (Philippians 4:19). We can pray this to God and ask Him to supply all our needs in Christ Jesus. After all, Paul wrote to the Ephesians: "Now to him who is able to do immeasurably more than all we ask or imagine, according to his power that is at work within us" (Ephesians 3:20). He is at work within us, through partnership with Him, through prayer, and He can do more than we could ever ask or imagine. But we should ask!

In our time of turmoil, in the midst of spiritual warfare, we must pray and call upon the name of the Lord. He will answer us and we will be *victorious*. We can continue interceding in prayer and praise God in advance for what we know He will do soon. "The persistent calling upon the Lord breaks through every stronghold of the devil, for nothing is impossible with God. For Christians in these troubled times there is simply no other way."² The writer of Hebrews encouraged us with perseverance, to keep our eyes focused on Jesus. "Therefore, since we are surrounded by such a great cloud of witnesses, let us throw off everything that hinders and the sin that so easily entangles. And let us **run with perseverance** the race marked out for us, fixing our eyes on Jesus, the pioneer and perfecter of faith" (Hebrews 12:1-2).

6 | PROMISES/PROPHECY

The sixth key to spiritual victory in spiritual warfare is to stand on *promises and prophecy*. We must stand on God's Word and His promises to have spiritual victory. We must declare those promises over our lives as we pursue victory in spiritual warfare. We can "prophesy the promises" over our lives in the middle of the fight. Remember, opposition gives opportunity if we approach the oppositional foes and moments in this way. In this context, battles are sometimes the best place to be.

Paul wrote to Timothy:

> Timothy, my son, I am giving you this command in keeping with the prophecies once made about you, so that by recalling them you may fight the battle well, holding on to faith and a good conscience, which some have rejected and so have suffered shipwreck with regard to the faith.
>
> —1 TIMOTHY 1:18-19

Paul was encouraging Timothy to hold on to the prophecies he spoke about him and recall them in the fight, in the battle, to keep the faith, and fight the good fight. Use the prophecies as a strong point, as a *weapon,* to win the victory. Paul also wrote to the Thessalonians: "Do not quench the Spirit. Do not treat prophecies with contempt but test them all; hold on to what is good, reject every kind of evil" (1 Thessalonians 5:19-22).

Peter spoke about this on Pentecost, while quoting the prophet Joel: "In the last days, God says, I will pour out my Spirit on all people. Your sons and daughters will prophesy, your young men will see visions, your old men will dream dreams" (Acts 2:17). Later Peter said, "and everyone who calls on the name of the Lord will be saved" (Acts 2:21). We should seek wisdom, discernment, and revelation from God. We should ask Him to reveal visions to us, His *vision* for us, to win in spiritual warfare. Remember, He is the God of miracles. James wrote: "You do not have, because you do not ask" (James 4:2). Ask Him for wisdom, discernment, revelation, vision, and He will answer. Proverbs says, "where there is no revelation, people cast off restraint; but blessed is the one who heeds wisdom's instruction" (Proverbs 29:18).

7 | POSITION/PASSION

The seventh and final key to spiritual victory in spiritual warfare is to understand our *position* and pursue *passion* in spiritual battles. First, what I mean by position is humility. James wrote: "God opposes the proud but shows favor to the humble" (James 4:6). Peter wrote: "Therefore, humble yourselves under the mighty hand of God, that He may exalt you in due time" (1 Peter 5:6 NKJV). Jesus said, "so the last will be first, and the first will be last" (Matthew 20:16). We must humble ourselves and surrender to Jesus. Jesus also said, "whoever wants to be my disciple must deny themselves and take up their cross daily and follow me. For whoever wants to save their life will lose it, but whoever loses their life for me will save it" (Luke 9:23-24).

Second, what I mean by position is that we are co-heirs with Christ and are, therefore, royalty. Not from anything we have done, but because of Christ's death on the Cross, restoring us into right relationship with God. God has adopted us as His children. As God's children, we are also co-heirs with Christ. Paul wrote: "Now if we are children, then we are heirs—heirs of God and co-heirs with Christ, if indeed we share in his sufferings in order that we may also share in his glory" (Romans 8:17). Peter wrote: "But you are a chosen people, a royal priesthood, a holy nation,

God's special possession, that you may declare the praises of him who called you out of darkness into his wonderful light" (1 Peter 2:9).

The other part to this section is to pursue passion in spiritual warfare. We must pursue Jesus and His plan for our life with passion. We must pursue not just our ambitions, but His mission for our life. Jim Cymbala wrote: "God will manifest himself in direct proportion to our passion for him."[1] In the famous passage called "The Great Commission," Jesus gave a final directive to His disciples, prior to His ascension. In that passage, He said, "therefore go and make disciples of all nations, baptizing them in the name of the Father and of the Son and of the Holy Spirit, and teaching them to obey everything I have commanded you" (Matthew 28:19-20). Mark's Gospel put it this way: "He said to them, 'go into all the world and preach the gospel to all creation'" (Mark 16:15). That, too, is the directive that Jesus gives to us. It is also one of the reasons I wrote this book, to share the Gospel and to teach.

One last key for spiritual victory on the concept of our position and pursing passion is "standing in the gap." This reminds me of the story of Esther. During this time in the Bible, in the Book of Esther, the Jewish people were living in exile in Persia, under King Xerxes. Esther was Jewish by descent and was chosen by Xerxes to be his queen. Through the crafty deceit of a man named Haman, he tricked King Xerxes into signing a decree to destroy the Jewish people in Esther 3. When Esther found out, she decided to approach the King to lobby for the lives of her people, but first, she needed to hear from God, so she planned a prayer and fast. She instructed them: "Do not eat or drink for three days, night or day. I and my attendants will fast as you do. When this is done, I will go to the king, even though it is against the law. And if I perish, I perish" (Esther 4:15-16).

We see that Esther was fasting and praying, and she was prepared to risk her life for her people. Esther then went boldly before the king and invited him to a banquet (see Esther 5:4). At the banquet, the king asked her "what is your request" (see Esther 7:2 NLT)? "Then Queen Esther answered, 'If I have found favor with you, Your Majesty, and if it pleases you, grant me my life—this is my petition. And spare my people—this is my request'" (Esther 7:3). King Xerxes granted her request to spare her life and her people. Haman was then killed for his deceit and treachery.

One of the classic lines from the book of Esther comes when her uncle Mordecai was trying to convince Esther to approach the king. Mordecai said to her, "and who knows but that you have come to your royal position for such a time as this" (Esther 4:14). She was placed in to her position, by God, for such a time as this, and she rose to the occasion. Because of Esther's boldness and faithfulness, she was triumphant, and her people were spared. We, too, must rise to the occasion as royalty and righteousness in God, through Christ, and we must stand in the gap, for such a time as this.

"When it comes to spiritual matters, you and I will never know our potential under God until we step out and take risks on the front line of battle. We will never see what power and anointing are possible until we bond with our King and go out in his name to establish his kingdom."[1]

I pray and hope this book was a blessing to you. I pray for

victory for you in spiritual warfare and for favor in your life. I will end with this verse from Numbers and I pray it blesses you as you go out as well: "The Lord bless you and keep you; the Lord make his face shine on you and be gracious to you; the Lord turn his face toward you and give you peace" (Numbers 6:24-26). Stand firm, win your battles, go into all the world and preach the Gospel, stand in the gap, the time is now!

EPILOGUE

In this book we explored what the Bible has to say about spiritual warfare. We examined "Spiritual Landscapes" in Part 1 (Valleys, Mountains, Wilderness, Exile), "Spiritual Oppression" in Part 2 (Fire, Giants, Storms), and "Spiritual Victory" in Part 3 (Prodigal, The Battle Within, The Armor of God, Victory). We walked through each of these areas to navigate landscapes, overcome oppression, and learn how to be victorious. In this epilogue, I hope to tie the whole book together for you and share some final, parting thoughts.

Eventually, breakthrough did come for me while writing this book and praying to overcome spiritual warfare in my own life. I'm still praying for other specific goals that I have and for victory in certain areas of my life. I believe breakthrough is coming in those areas as well. Through the process of writing this book, God walked me personally through the spiritual landscapes in my life. He then subsequently showed me how to overcome spiritual oppression and achieve spiritual victory and what to share with you specifically on these topics. I hope as you read through these chapters and my stories you were able to relate, and I hope they help you in your own life.

Through the process of writing this book, God revealed to me a couple of overarching themes. One of the themes was pretty evident from the beginning of the process and it also headlined the last part of the book, which was *victory.* We fight *from* victory not just *for* victory, because of Jesus Christ. He won the war, but we are still fighting the daily spiritual battles in our lives. We are in hand-to-hand combat against the enemy. We must go in the strength of Christ, put on the armor of God, and use the concepts in this book to overcome the evil one. We must use the Word of God to be victorious. We must fight *from* victory in our lives and in the lives of our loved ones.

The other overarching theme for the book came to me at the end of the process and God made it clear that He wanted me to tie in the "war of words" and the importance of "speaking" in spiritual warfare. Since it is a "war of words," then the enemy is speaking. If he can't intimidate us out of the fight, then he will attack us with words. We discussed at length that the Devil is the accuser, liar, and deceiver. "The Devil prowls around like a roaring lion looking for someone to devour" (see 1 Peter 5:8). He is roaring and he is speaking, trying to intimidate us with the roar and use his words to fight us. As he is speaking, he hopes we are listening and will run from the fight. But we have to speak back, and really, we have to roar back. Proverbs says, "the wicked flee though no one pursues, but the righteous are as bold as a lion" (Proverbs 28:1). We must be bold as lions. We must start speaking back against the enemy and speak life over ourselves, our families, and others.

Let's review some of the main stories from the book and see how they tie into this overarching theme of *war of words* and the importance of *speaking* in spiritual warfare and for overall spiritual victory in our lives. Ezekiel in the valley of dry bones, after getting a word from God, then "prophesied to the dry bones and prophesied to the breath" (see Ezekiel 37). At the direction of God, Ezekiel was *speaking*. After praying to God, Jesus called Lazarus out of his tomb. "Jesus called in a loud voice, 'Lazarus, come out!' The dead man came out, his hands and feet wrapped with strips of linen, and a cloth around his face. Jesus said to them, 'Take off the grave clothes and let him go'" (John 11:43-44). Jesus was *speaking* and called dry bones to *life*. He called that which was dead to life, to glorify the Father. Since we are created in the Image of God, the One who speaks life, we must also learn to speak life!

After getting a word in the prophetic realm, Elijah told King Ahab to "go, eat and drink, for there is the sound of a heavy rain" and then Elijah told his servant to "go and look toward the sea" (see 1 Kings 18). At the direction of God and the Holy Spirit, in the spiritual realm, Elijah was *speaking* prophetically into the natural; the rain came, the drought ended, and the miracle happened.

We saw in the Book of Exodus, that the children of Israel were supposed to go on to the Promised Land, but complaining, poor attitudes, and lack of faith in God cost them 40 years in the wilderness. Subsequently they listened to the ten spies' fears over Caleb and Joshua's desire to enter the Promised Land and defeat the giants (see Numbers 13). The ten spies' *words* cost the entire generation of Israelites their destiny. However, later in life, Joshua, got a word from God and took the next generation into the Promised Land (see Joshua Chapters 1 - 3). God encouraged Joshua to keep the Word "always on your lips; meditate on it day and night" (Joshua 1:8). We must *speak* the Word always.

Daniel's prayers landed him in the lions' den, but "God

sent his angel, and he shut the mouths of the lions" (Daniel 6:22) and later Daniel's prayer awarded an encounter with an angel who said, "your words were heard, and I have come in response to them" (Daniel 10:12). In the face of death and in response to prayer, God showed up. In another chapter, Daniel's friends, Shadrach, Meshach and Abednego, told King Nebuchadnezzar after being threatened with death: "If we are thrown into the blazing furnace, the God we serve is able to deliver us from it, and he will deliver us from Your Majesty's hand" (Daniel 3:17). In the face of a tyrant king and imminent fiery death, they were *speaking*, and they were delivered.

David had already defeated his own lion in the field as a shepherd. Now faced with a battle against Goliath, David said, "you come against me with sword and spear and javelin, but I come against you in the name of the Lord Almighty, the God of the armies of Israel, whom you have defied. This day the Lord will deliver you into my hands, and I'll strike you down and cut off you head" (1 Samuel 17:45-46). In the face of a giant enemy, David was *speaking*, and He won. While being tempted and tested in the wilderness by the Devil, Jesus established victory by speaking Scripture. In the face of the Devil, Jesus was *speaking*, and He won (see Matthew 4).

While in the innermost cell of a dungeon, despite being beaten and shackled, awaiting their fate from the authorities, Paul and Silas began "praying and singing hymns to God" (Acts 16:25) and "the prison doors flew open, and everyone's chains came loose" (Acts 16:26). In the face of the enemy, Paul and Silas were *speaking and praising*.

In a later story, Paul got a word from an angel of God

while in a storm on a ship in the face of imminent demise. He wrote: "Last night an angel of the God to whom I belong and whom I serve stood beside me and said, 'Do not be afraid, Paul. You must stand trial before Caesar; and God has graciously given you the lives of all who sail with you'" (Acts 27:23-24). Then Paul spoke to them, "so, keep up your courage, men, for I have faith in God that it will happen just as he told me. Nevertheless, we must run aground on some island" (Acts 27:25-26). In the face of the storm and in the face of death, Paul was *speaking*.

In "The Armor of God" chapter we looked at the offensive weapons of the Sword of the Spirit, which is the Word of God, and the spear or javelin of prayer. Both of these offensive weapons require *speaking*. Remember the Word of God here is the Rhema Word or the spoken Word of God. We also discussed the spiritual strategies of strengthening and speaking our faith and leaning on God for victory and breakthrough. These strategies include: "praise before the breakthrough," "worship before the worry," "prophesy the promise," and "thank Him before you see the outcome." As discussed, to employ these strategies we must first get a word from God, most commonly directly from Scripture, and stand on it and *speak it forth*.

Paul wrote to the Romans about spiritual gifts or motivations, such as "prophesying, serving, teaching, encouraging, giving, leading, and showing mercy" (See Romans 12:6-8). If we study them closely, we see that many of them require *speaking* to operate in the gift. Similarly, regarding the works of service and ministries, Paul wrote to the Ephesians: "So Christ himself gave the apostles, the prophets, the evangelists, the pastors and teachers, to equip his people for works of service, so that the body of Christ may be built up" (Ephesians 4:11-12). Most or all of these require *speaking* as a part of the service.

We discussed previously that salvation requires *speaking* or professing with your mouth: "For it is with your heart that you believe and are justified, and it is with your mouth that you profess your faith and are saved" (Romans 10:10). Salvation and faith are activated by *speaking* out our beliefs. We must be resolved in those beliefs and stand firm against the enemy. What we do with Jesus Christ, who we believe and profess Him to be, determines where we will spend eternity! Paul also wrote about *speaking* or preaching to others so that they too can hear and believe:

> How, then, can they call on the one they have not believed in? And how can they believe in the one of whom they have not heard? And how can they hear without someone preaching to them? And how can anyone preach unless they are sent? As it is written: "How beautiful are the feet of those who bring good news!"
>
> —ROMANS 10:14-15

Just after this, Paul wrote: "Consequently, faith comes from hearing the message, and the message is heard through the word about Christ" (Romans 10:17). Therefore, we are encouraged to share the message, the good news about Jesus Christ, and that requires *speaking* or preaching.

We saw that the mind is not just a piece in the chess game, but it is the entire chessboard. Battles in the mind are won by resisting the enemy and winning the *war of words*, through power in the name of Jesus. Jesus is the Lion of Judah and Judah means praise. Jesus is also the Lamb and remember that we triumph by the blood of the lamb and by the word of our testimony (about the lamb). May we win the *war of words* against the enemy by speaking back and may we flourish in the Kingdom of God while speaking life over ourselves, our families, and others.

NOTES

Chapter 1: We Are at War
1. C.S. Lewis, *The Weight of Glory* (New York: HarperCollins), 2015.

Chapter 3: Mountains
1. Jentezen Franklin, *The Power of the Lord's Table*, Web Sermon. Accessed Jan 2020.
2. Jim Cymbala, *Fresh Wind, Fresh Fire* (Grand Rapids: Zondervan, 2018), 117.

Chapter 4: Wilderness
1. "Wilderness". Merriam-Webster.com. Web. Accessed December 2019.
2. Jim Cymbala, *Fresh Wind, Fresh Fire* (Grand Rapids: Zondervan, 2018), 184.
3. John Bevere, *How God Prepares You for Change*, Web. Accessed January 2020.

Chapter 5: Exile
1. "Exile". Merriam-Webster.com. Web. Accessed December 2019.
2. "Revelation". Dictionary.com. Web. Accessed December 2019.

Chapter 7: Giants:
1. Greg Laurie. *Facing Giants in the New Year*. Web Sermon. Accessed Jan 2020.

Chapter 9: Prodigal

1. "Prodigal". Merriam-Webster.com. Web. Accessed January 2020.
2. "Kezazah". Encyclopedia.com/religion/. Web. Accessed February 2020.

Chapter 10: The Battle Within

1. "Sanctification". Dictionary.com. Web. Accessed January 2020.
2. Jentezen Franklin, *Fasting* (Lake Mary: Charisma House, 2008), 224, 225.

Chapter 11: Armor of God:

1. Ron DiCianni. *Spiritual Warfare*. Painting referenced.

Chapter 12: Victory

1. Jim Cymbala, *Fresh Wind, Fresh Fire* (Grand Rapids: Zondervan), 2018, 175, 183.
2. Jentezen Franklin, *The Power of the Lord's Table*, Web Sermon. Accessed Jan 2020.

ACKNOWLEDGEMENTS

First and foremost, I want to thank God and acknowledge the work of Christ throughout my life. He has blessed me with His grace, mercy, and unfailing love. He gave me revelation to write this book and ultimately guided me on what to say and how to say it. I am eternally grateful for His Word and I am humbled and honored to be able to write about it and share my thoughts with the world.

To my amazing wife, Emily, thank you for your love, support, and encouragement through the book writing process and throughout the entire project, even to the very end. Thank you for giving of your time, energy, and effort through the countless hours you spent to help me carry this book to the finish line. The final product is what it is in huge part because of you!

To my parents and family, thank you for your constant source of encouragement and for always believing in me. So many choices and moving parts in a project like this and your wisdom and the ability to use you all as a sounding board was extremely helpful. A special thank you to my father, Ron, for your help with learning about website development, marketing and all the intricacies that come with it. To my father-in-law, Pete, thank you for reviewing the manuscript, your advice, wisdom, and for writing one of the "praises" for the book.

To my closest friends who have walked this journey alongside me. You have not only shaped this book but the person who wrote it. To Sam, thank you for your friendship, wisdom, and insightful suggestions for the manuscript. I appreciate your meetings, prayers, pastoral input, and for writing one of the "praises" for the book.

To Pastor Jamie, thank you for all of your prayers and much-needed encouragement in the early stages of writing this book. Pastor Brandon, thank you for reviewing the manuscript and for your theological assessment and feedback.

To Aubrey, thank you for your input and generous assistance on manuscript writing and the publishing process. You were immensely helpful in guiding me through the complex process of book publishing. I wish you all the success on your newly released book and future endeavors!

To Victoria, thank you for doing the book cover design, manuscript formatting, advertising, and for all of your creative ideas and input. Thank you for your attention to detail and aspiration for excellence. You are extremely talented at what you do!

To Bobby, thank you for doing my photoshoot for the book cover and website! Thank you for sharing your creative ideas, brilliant talent and skills with me. I wish you and Victoria the utmost success and favor in both of your careers.

To my readers, I am honored, grateful, and humbled that you would buy and read my book. I appreciate your support more than you even know! You are a child of God and are deeply loved. In the face of spiritual warfare, it is my prayer that this book will help you stand firm... pray fervently...and hope without measure. With God, we can overcome the enemy!

ABOUT THE AUTHOR

NEVIN WHITE is a doctor, author, and entrepreneur. He completed his residency training at In His Image, a faith-based program with a mission to serve God through medicine. He co-founded and practices medicine at Compassion Family Medicine and Doctor Online Oklahoma. He has a passion for helping people improve their health in all aspects of their lives, including mind, body, and spirit. He and his wife, Emily, and their two Labrador retrievers, Lucy and Abby, make their home in Tulsa, Oklahoma.

To connect with Nevin go to NevinWhite.com.

Made in the USA
Columbia, SC
09 June 2020